THE FATHER

UNVEILING THE UNTOLD SACRIFICES OF A SILENT HERO

DR P NIDHEESH

Made with ♥ on the Notion Press Platform
www.notionpress.com

To my dearest father,

You are the pillar of strength, the guiding light, and the embodiment of unconditional love. This book is dedicated to you, my real-life hero, who has shaped me into the person I am today. You have been my rock, my mentor, and my source of inspiration throughout my journey.

From the very beginning, you instilled in me the values of integrity, compassion, and perseverance. You taught me to dream big, to believe in myself, and to never be afraid of the challenges that life presents. Your unwavering support and belief in my abilities have propelled me forward, giving me the courage to pursue my dreams and overcome obstacles along the way.

I am privileged to have witnessed your unwavering dedication to our family. You worked tirelessly, sacrificing your own needs and desires, to ensure that we had every opportunity to thrive. You selflessly put our needs above your own, tirelessly juggling the responsibilities of work, family, and personal growth.

You taught me the importance of responsibility and the value of hard work. Through your example, I learned the significance of balancing the demands of life while never losing sight of what truly matters. Your tireless efforts and sacrifices have laid the foundation for my own success and have taught me the true meaning of resilience and determination.

But beyond the tangible achievements and material accomplishments, it is your unwavering love, support, and presence that have had the greatest impact on my life. You have been there in my moments of triumph and celebration, offering words of encouragement and pride. And you have been there in my moments of despair and doubt, offering a comforting embrace and the reassurance that I am never alone.

You have shown me the power of connection, the strength of compassion, and the beauty of a love that knows no bounds. Your love has nurtured my soul, giving me the confidence to navigate the world with grace and kindness.

In every aspect of my life, I see your influence. As a successful Homoeopathic practitioner, I owe my passion for healing and my dedication to helping others to your unwavering belief in the power of empathy and compassion. Your guidance has shaped my approach to life, my way of thinking, and my unwavering commitment to making a positive impact in the world.

I am eternally grateful to have you as my father, my mentor, and my friend. In this book, I aim to shed light on the often unnoticed sufferings of fathers, to honour their sacrifices, and to offer a heartfelt tribute to the extraordinary fathers like you who have shaped our lives.

Thank you, dear father, for everything you have done and continue to do. You are my greatest blessing, and I am forever grateful for the privilege of being your child. May this book serve as a testament to the profound impact you have had on my life and the lives of so many others.

With all my love and gratitude,

Dr P Nidheesh

Contents

Contents

Preface

In the quiet moments before embarking on the journey of a book, there exists a sacred space of reflection—a space where memories, emotions, and stories intertwine to create a tapestry of human experience. It is within this space that I find myself as I pen these words—a preface to a book that seeks to illuminate the often unnoticed sufferings, sacrifices, and unspoken duties of fathers.

As I reflect upon my own journey as a writer and as a son, I am filled with a deep sense of purpose—an earnest desire to shed light on the profound experiences of fatherhood. For too long, the role of fathers has been overshadowed, their contributions downplayed, and their struggles left unspoken. It is time to change the narrative, to offer a platform for their stories to be heard and acknowledged.

This book is not just a collection of words on a page; it is a labour of love, an ode to the fathers who have shaped our lives in countless ways. It is an exploration of the complexities, joys, and challenges that accompany the journey of fatherhood—a journey that often goes unnoticed and unappreciated.

Through heartfelt narratives, I aim to capture the multifaceted nature of fatherhood. I strive to evoke empathy, understanding, and a deeper connection between the readers and the fathers whose stories unfold within these pages. It is my hope that these stories will resonate with readers from all walks of life, transcending cultural, societal, and personal boundaries.

In writing this book, I have been both a witness and a conduit for the emotions, experiences, and untold stories of fathers. I have listened to their voices, heard their struggles, and felt their unwavering love. It is a humbling privilege to share their narratives and to offer a glimpse into the inner world of fatherhood—a world that is often shrouded in silence.

I extend my deepest gratitude to all the fathers who have shared their stories, their vulnerabilities, and their triumphs with me. Your willingness to open your hearts and allow your experiences to be captured in these words is a testament to your bravery and strength. I am forever grateful for the opportunity to honour your journey through this book.

To the readers, I invite you to join me on this odyssey—a journey that unravels the layers of a father's story, one that reaches beyond the surface to touch the very depths of our shared humanity. Together, let us bear witness to the sufferings, sacrifices, and resilience of fathers, and let us emerge with a deeper understanding and appreciation for their invaluable role in our lives.

With heartfelt anticipation,
Dr P Nidheesh

Acknowledgements

Writing a book is not a solitary endeavour; it is the result of the collective support, guidance, and inspiration from those who have touched our lives. In expressing my heartfelt gratitude, I would like to acknowledge the following individuals whose contributions have been instrumental in bringing this book to life.

First and foremost, I want to express my deepest appreciation to my father, the source of inspiration for this book. Your unwavering love, sacrifices, and teachings have shaped my perspective on fatherhood and have fueled my passion to shed light on the unspoken journey of fathers. Thank you for being my guiding light and for instilling in me the values that form the foundation of this book.

To my family, thank you for your love, patience, and unwavering support throughout this writing journey. Your belief in me and your understanding of the time and effort required for this project have meant the world to me. Your encouragement and presence have been a constant source of motivation, and I am forever grateful for your unwavering support.

I would like to extend my gratitude to my friends and colleagues who have provided valuable insights, encouragement, and feedback during the writing process. Your support and willingness to listen to my ideas and thoughts have enriched this book and made it a collaborative endeavour.

A special thank you to the countless fathers who shared their stories, experiences, and vulnerabilities with me. Your willingness to open your hearts and trust me with your narratives is truly humbling.

I am immensely grateful to my editor, whose keen eye, guidance, and expertise have helped shape this book into its final form. Your insights, suggestions, and attention to detail have elevated the quality of the writing, and I am deeply appreciative of your dedication to this project.

I would also like to express my gratitude to the publishing team who have worked tirelessly behind the scenes to bring this book to life. Your professionalism, expertise, and commitment to excellence have been invaluable in turning my vision into a reality.

Lastly, I want to thank the readers who have chosen to embark on this journey with me. Your openness, curiosity, and willingness to explore the stories and experiences of fathers are what make this book meaningful. It is my sincere hope that this book resonates with you, evokes empathy, and fosters a deeper understanding and appreciation for the unsung heroes of fatherhood.

In writing this acknowledgement, I am reminded of the countless individuals who have played a role in shaping my life and this book. Though I cannot name each one individually, please know that your influence and support have not gone unnoticed, and I am forever grateful.

With heartfelt appreciation,

Dr P Nidheesh

Prologue

Welcome to the extraordinary journey of Fatherhood. In the pages that follow, we start on a profound exploration of the untold story of a father's sacrifices and resilience. It is an invitation to delve deep into the heart of fatherhood, uncovering the extraordinary feats performed by fathers every day, often without recognition or fanfare.

Like any journey, this book is a pathway that winds through the emotional landscapes of fatherhood. It is a pilgrimage that seeks to touch the very essence of what it means to be a father. It is a narrative that reaches out, not to the intellect, but straight to the heart, evoking empathy and compassion.

Throughout history, the focus has predominantly been on the mother's role in raising a child. The unique struggles and sacrifices of fathers have remained hidden in the shadows, overshadowed by societal expectations and ingrained stereotypes. But within the depths of fatherhood lies an untold story, waiting to be unravelled, waiting to be heard.

With each turn of the page, we unveil the layers of a father's sacrifices—both seen and unseen. We traverse the emotional landscapes, navigating the joys and challenges that intertwine in the tapestry of fatherhood. We bear witness to the silent battles fought, the burdens carried, and the unspoken sacrifices made for the sake of a family.

We invite you to step into the shoes of fathers from all walks of life, to understand their experiences, and to appreciate the profound impact they have on their children and families.

Prepare to encounter the tender moments of holding a newborn in one's arms for the first time—the overwhelming love that washes over a father's heart. But also, be prepared to witness the fears and doubts that creep in, the sleepless nights spent tending to a crying child, and the quiet moments of self-doubt that only a father truly knows.

Unveiling Societal Shadows:

Society has long perpetuated the image of the stoic and unyielding father figure—the rock upon which families find support. Yet, within the depths of a father's soul resides a vulnerability that defies expectations. It is in this vulnerability that we discover the heart of a father—a heart capable of boundless love, immense joy, and unspoken fears.

In the pages that follow, we invite you to embrace this vulnerability, to witness the beauty that emerges when walls are lowered and authentic emotions are allowed to flow.

As we are on this journey, let us shed the notion that vulnerability equates to weakness. Instead, let us recognize it as a wellspring of courage—a testament to the strength required to embrace the complexities of fatherhood. It is through vulnerability that fathers connect with their children on a profound level, forging lifelong bonds that shape the very fabric of their lives.

In the moments of vulnerability, a father reveals his deepest fears and insecurities—worries that he may not measure up, doubts that he may falter, and the weight of responsibility that rests upon his shoulders. It is within these shared vulnerabilities that we find common ground, transcending societal divides and forging connections rooted in empathy and compassion.

As we delve into the stories of fathers, prepare to witness the joys that kindle their hearts—the uncontainable laughter, the tears of pride, and the overwhelming love that permeates their very being. But also be prepared to witness their struggles—the sleepless nights spent tending to a sick child, the moments of self-doubt that cloud their minds, and the sacrifices made silently to provide for their loved ones.

A Symphony of Sacrifices

Fathers are often seen as the sturdy pillars, providing stability and strength to their families. Yet, beneath the surface, there exists a shade of sacrifices woven intricately into the fabric of a father's life. These sacrifices are not grand gestures but are found in the quiet moments, the everyday choices, and the relentless commitment to their loved ones.

In this journey, we peel back the layers, revealing the profound impact of a father's sacrifices. We delve into the depths of their roles as providers, protectors, and mentors, uncovering the countless hours spent away from their families, the dreams set aside, and the personal aspirations sacrificed to create a better life for those they hold dear.

As we listen to the symphony of sacrifices, we come to understand that a father's duty extends far beyond financial provision. We witness the emotional labour invested in nurturing and guiding their children, the sleepless nights spent worrying, and the delicate balancing act between work and family that often takes a toll on their own well-being.

In this exploration, we seek to honour the unspoken duties of fathers—the sacrifices made without expectation of recognition or reward. We invite you to listen to the melodies of love and selflessness that resound within the hearts of fathers, capturing the essence of their dedication and the depth of their commitment.We recognize that their sacrifices are not diminished by their silence but are magnified by the profound depth of their actions.

As we traverse on this journey together, let us cast aside preconceived notions and open our hearts to the universal truths of fatherhood. Let us celebrate the sacrifices and resilience of fathers, for they are the unsung heroes of our families, shaping the lives of generations to come.

So, dear reader, take my hand and let us step into the uncharted territory of a father's journey. Through the triumphs and trials, the joys and sorrows, we will walk this path together, gaining a deeper understanding and appreciation for the silent sacrifices that fathers make. Let us uncover their stories, embrace their humanity, and honour their unwavering dedication.

This is our journey—a journey of empathy, compassion, and profound discovery. Together, we will unravel the untold story of a father's sacrifices and resilience, forever transforming our understanding of fatherhood.

CHAPTER ONE

EMOTIONAL STRUGGLES

In this poignant chapter, 'The Father' delves into the emotional landscape of fatherhood, uncovering the hidden struggles that fathers often bear silently. It explores the depths of their emotions, the inner battles fought behind closed doors, and the profound impact these struggles have on their lives and relationships. Through raw and honest narratives, the chapter shines a light on the vulnerability, resilience, and immense strength required to navigate the complex emotions that come with being a father. It invites readers to witness the emotional journey of fathers, fostering empathy, understanding, and a deeper connection with their own fathers or father figures. This chapter sets the stage for an emotional exploration of fatherhood, laying the foundation for the transformative journey that unfolds throughout the book.

His Struggles

In the realm of fatherhood, a profound journey unfolds—a journey that transcends time and resonates with fathers everywhere. It is a journey of sacrifices, resilience, and untold struggles that often go unnoticed, but touch the hearts of fathers across generations.

Every day, fathers rise to the challenges before them, driven by an unyielding love for their families. They navigate the voyage of family life, shouldering responsibilities that extend far beyond mere provision. They become anchors, protectors, and guiding lights for their children and loved ones.

Behind their strong exteriors, fathers bear burdens that often remain unseen. They carry the weight of unspoken worries and fears, wrestling with self-doubt and the pressure to be everything their family needs. They hide their vulnerability, wearing a mask of strength to shield their loved ones from the depth of their own struggles.

In the pursuit of their family's well-being, fathers willingly set aside their own dreams, ambitions, and desires. They sacrifice sleep, personal time, and leisure, pouring their energy into creating a nurturing and secure environment for their children to thrive.

Through the challenges they face, fathers silently battle internal conflicts. They strive to find the delicate balance between their roles as caregivers, providers, and individuals with their own needs and aspirations. It is a constant dance of selflessness and self-discovery, navigating the complexities of identity within the context of fatherhood.

In the quiet moments, fathers grapple with the weight of societal expectations. They challenge traditional notions of masculinity, seeking to redefine fatherhood on their own terms. They long to express their emotions openly, to break free from the shackles of stoicism, and to create a culture where vulnerability is embraced and understood.

Yet, amidst the trials and tribulations, fathers find solace in the power of connection. They forge unbreakable bonds with their children, weaving a curtain of love, guidance, and unwavering support. They become the pillars upon which their families lean, the sounding boards for dreams and fears, and the providers of unconditional love.

Through it all, fathers yearn for understanding, appreciation, and recognition. They are the silent heroes, the unsung champions of fatherhood who persevere, sacrificing their own well-being for the sake of their families. Their journey is one of depth, complexity, and immeasurable love.

In the quiet corners of a father's heart lie struggles that often remain unseen, etched in the very fibres of his being. These struggles weave their way into his journey, shaping his experiences and leaving an indelible mark on his soul.

As a father, he grapples with the weight of responsibility that rests upon his shoulders. The pressures of providing for his family, ensuring their well-being, and guiding them through the complexities of life can be overwhelming. He navigates the challenges of balancing work and family, striving to be present and attentive despite the demands of a fast-paced world.

In the depths of his heart, he battles the fears that haunt him in the stillness of the night. The fear of not being enough, of failing to meet the expectations he sets for himself. He questions his abilities as a father, wondering if he is making the right decisions, if he is guiding his children on the right path.

Amidst the struggles, he confronts his own vulnerability—the emotions that surge within him, often tempered by the societal expectation to be strong and stoic. He learns to conceal his fears, his doubts, and his own need for support, donning a mask of strength to shield his loved ones from the depths of his inner battles.

In the face of adversity, he confronts the challenges that life presents. He may face financial hardships, career setbacks, or personal losses, all while maintaining a brave front for the sake of his family. He navigates through these storms, weathering them with unwavering resilience, even when his own heart may feel fragile.

Yet, within the struggle lies a resolute determination—a fire that burns within him to overcome obstacles and provide a better life for his children. He sacrifices his own desires, dreams, and sometimes even his own well-being, in order to create a safe and nurturing environment where his children can flourish.

Amidst the struggles, he seeks solace and support. He recognizes the importance of connection and finds strength in the bonds he shares with his loved ones. He learns to lean on his partner, to seek guidance and understanding from trusted friends, and to cultivate a support network that can uplift him in times of need.

And through it all, in the depths of his struggle, he discovers the beauty and joy that fatherhood brings. He witnesses the milestones, both big and small, that mark his children's growth. He cherishes the laughter, the hugs, and the moments of pure love that make every struggle worthwhile.

In his struggle, he finds growth and transformation. He evolves as a person, learning from his mistakes and embracing the lessons life teaches him. He finds resilience, courage, and an unwavering love that knows no bounds.

For within the struggles of a father lies a journey of self-discovery, sacrifice, and unwavering commitment. It is a journey that may go unnoticed by many, but its impact reverberates through generations. It is a journey that shapes lives, nurtures souls, and leaves an enduring legacy of love.

His Responsibility - The Weight of the life

In the complicated dance of fatherhood, one of the greatest struggles a father faces is the weight of responsibility. It is a delicate balancing act, where he strives to fulfil his duties as a provider, caretaker, and nurturer while also tending to his own needs and aspirations.

The demands of work can be relentless, requiring long hours and unwavering dedication. He may face the pressure of climbing the corporate ladder, striving to create a better future for his loved ones. But in doing so, he grapples with the challenge of carving out time for his family, fearing that his presence may be overshadowed by the demands of his career.

Amidst the demands of work, the father yearns to be present for his family—to share in the joys and triumphs, to offer guidance and support, and to create lasting memories. He strives to find the delicate balance between being physically present and emotionally available, recognizing the importance of quality time and meaningful connections. Yet, it is a constant struggle, a juggling act that requires careful planning and prioritisation.

In the midst of this balancing act, the father also confronts the need to care for himself. He recognizes that self-care is not selfish but essential for his well-being and the well-being of his family. However, finding time for personal pursuits and nurturing his own passions becomes a challenge amidst the whirlwind of responsibilities. He must carve out moments to recharge, to pursue hobbies, and to cultivate his own growth and fulfilment.

The weight of responsibility can sometimes lead to feelings of guilt. The father may question whether he is doing enough, whether he is truly present for his family, or if he is sacrificing too much of himself in the process. He must learn to navigate the intricacies of guilt, to find a sense of balance and self-compassion, and to understand that being a father does not mean being perfect but rather showing up with love, dedication, and authenticity.

Amidst the struggle, the father seeks support and understanding. He leans on his partner, sharing the load and collaborating in the journey of parenthood. He seeks the wisdom and guidance of fellow fathers, forming a community of support that provides solace, reassurance, and a shared understanding of the challenges they face.

In the quest to balance work, family, and self, the father embarks on a journey of self-discovery and growth. He learns to prioritise what truly matters, to let go of perfectionism, and to embrace the imperfections and uncertainties of fatherhood. He discovers the power of being present, of showing up with love and authenticity, and of creating meaningful connections with his children.

Ultimately, the weight of responsibility becomes a catalyst for personal transformation. The father learns to navigate the delicate tightrope, recognizing that the balance may shift and sway, but his unwavering commitment remains steadfast. He finds resilience in the face of challenges, strength in vulnerability, and a deep sense of fulfilment in witnessing the growth and happiness of his family.

His Identity and Selfhood

In the vast landscape of fatherhood, there exists an unspoken struggle—the delicate pursuit of balance between one's individual identity and the all-encompassing responsibilities of raising a child. As a father, navigating this profound journey becomes an exploration of selfhood, an introspective quest to understand who he is, who he aspires to be, and how he can harmonise his own dreams and aspirations with the intricate dynamics of family life.

In the depths of his soul, the father grapples with the evolving facets of his identity. The challenge lies in finding the equilibrium between fulfilling the needs of his family and nurturing his own personal growth. He yearns to carve out moments to pursue his interests, to cultivate his talents, and to preserve a sense of self amidst the whirlwind of parental responsibilities.

The father's journey towards balance is marked by moments of introspection and self-reflection. He questions his own desires and dreams, contemplating how they align with the greater tapestry of his family's needs and aspirations. It is a delicate dance between selflessness and self-discovery, where he strives to honour his own authenticity while creating a harmonious environment for his children to flourish.

As he navigates the labyrinth of identity, the father may encounter societal expectations that impose narrow definitions of masculinity and fatherhood. He challenges these preconceptions, forging his own path and redefining what it means to be a father. He embraces the opportunity to model emotional intelligence, vulnerability, and compassion, dismantling societal barriers and opening doors for a new paradigm of fatherhood.

In the pursuit of balance, the father discovers that it is not a static destination but a continuous journey. It requires adaptability, flexibility, and a willingness to recalibrate as circumstances evolve. It is about finding harmony, not perfection, and allowing space for growth and self-compassion along the way.

Through the intricate navigation of identity and selfhood, the father emerges as a multifaceted individual—an embodiment of love, growth, and resilience. He becomes a role model, not only for his children but for society at large, challenging traditional norms and embracing the power of authenticity. In weaving his own dreams into the fabric of family life, he creates an ocean of love, acceptance, and self-discovery that enriches the lives of his loved ones.

His Silent Battles

In the depths of a father's heart, there are silent battles fought—those of loss, grief, and change. Life's inevitable twists and turns bring forth moments of profound sadness, challenging the very fabric of his being. In these moments, he learns to cope, to heal, and to find strength amidst the shadows.

Loss casts its heavy veil upon the father's soul. Whether it be the loss of a loved one, the dissolution of a relationship, or the shattering of dreams, grief seeps into his heart. It envelops him in a cloak of sorrow, leaving him to navigate a landscape of emptiness and longing. Yet, within the depths of this darkness, he discovers the resilience to face each day, to honour the memories of what once was, and to seek solace in the love that remains.

Grief becomes his constant companion, an unwelcome guest that lingers in the corners of his mind. It visits unexpectedly, triggering waves of sadness and aching for what has been lost. But the father learns to embrace grief as a testament to the depth of his love. He finds solace in acknowledging his emotions, in allowing tears to flow freely, and in seeking support from loved ones who understand the weight of his pain.

Change, too, weaves its intricate threads into the shades of a father's life. It brings upheaval, unsettling the familiar rhythms and routines. The father must adapt, recalibrate, and find a new sense of normalcy. He grapples with the uncertainties that change brings—adjusting to new roles, forging different paths, and embracing the unknown. Yet, in the face of change, he discovers his own resilience and the capacity to grow amidst adversity.

In honouring the silent battles of fathers, we recognize their capacity to endure, to heal, and to rise above adversity. We offer our support and understanding, creating a space where they can openly express their grief, loss, and struggles. And in doing so, we acknowledge the indomitable spirit that resides within them, inspiring us all to face our own battles with grace, resilience, and an unwavering determination to find light in the midst of darkness.

Embossing of Societal Expectation over Him

Societal expectations cast a long shadow upon the realm of fatherhood, perpetuating stereotypes that can hinder a father's journey. These stereotypes, deeply ingrained in cultural norms and perceptions, create rigid expectations that limit the expression of fatherly love and involvement. Let us delve into these stereotypes, examining their impact and the ways in which fathers can challenge and overcome them.

The Provider Stereotype: One prevalent stereotype is that of the father as the sole provider for his family. This archetype assumes that his primary role is to be the breadwinner, focusing solely on financial responsibilities while neglecting emotional and domestic duties. This stereotype disregards the evolving dynamics of modern families, where shared responsibilities and gender equality have become central tenets. Fathers find themselves constrained by these expectations, often feeling pressure to prioritise work over family, sacrificing meaningful connections and shared responsibilities in the process.

The Distant and Emotionally Reserved Father: Another pervasive stereotype depicts fathers as emotionally distant and reserved. Society often expects fathers to embody stoicism, suppressing their emotions and expressing a limited range of feelings. This stereotype not only restricts the father's own emotional well-being but also hinders the development of close relationships with their children. By adhering to this stereotype, fathers may inadvertently create barriers to open communication and miss out on the opportunity to form deep and meaningful connections with their children.

The Incompetent Caregiver: Society often perpetuates the notion that fathers are inherently less capable or competent in caregiving and nurturing roles. This stereotype undermines a father's ability to be actively involved in their children's lives, portraying them as secondary caregivers or mere helpers rather than equal partners in parenting. As a result, fathers may face barriers in accessing resources and support systems that can aid in their journey as caregivers, limiting their potential to foster strong bonds and contribute to their children's well-being.

The Absent Father: One of the most damaging stereotypes is that of the absent father, painting a picture of fathers who are disengaged, uninvolved, or absent from their children's lives. While there are indeed instances where fathers are physically absent, this stereotype unfairly taints all fathers with a broad brush. It undermines the vast number of fathers who are deeply committed, present, and actively engaged in raising their children. By perpetuating this stereotype, society overlooks the immense impact that engaged fathers can have on their children's development, well-being, and overall happiness.

Challenging these stereotypes is a vital step towards creating a more inclusive and equitable vision of fatherhood. Fathers must reclaim their role as multifaceted individuals capable of nurturing, emotional expression, and active involvement. By actively challenging societal expectations, fathers can embrace their own unique journey, redefining what it means to be a father in the modern world.

Fathers can start by defying the provider stereotype and striving for a healthy work-life balance that allows them to prioritise family and emotional connection. By nurturing their own well-being and seeking support, fathers can break free from the emotional reserve stereotype, allowing themselves to authentically express their emotions and forge deeper connections with their children.

Actively engaging in caregiving and domestic responsibilities challenges the notion of fathers as incompetent caregivers. By sharing responsibilities, fathers can foster a sense of equality and partnership, creating a nurturing environment where children thrive. Fathers who actively participate in their children's lives, regardless of traditional gender roles, challenge the absent father stereotype, proving that love and involvement know no boundaries.

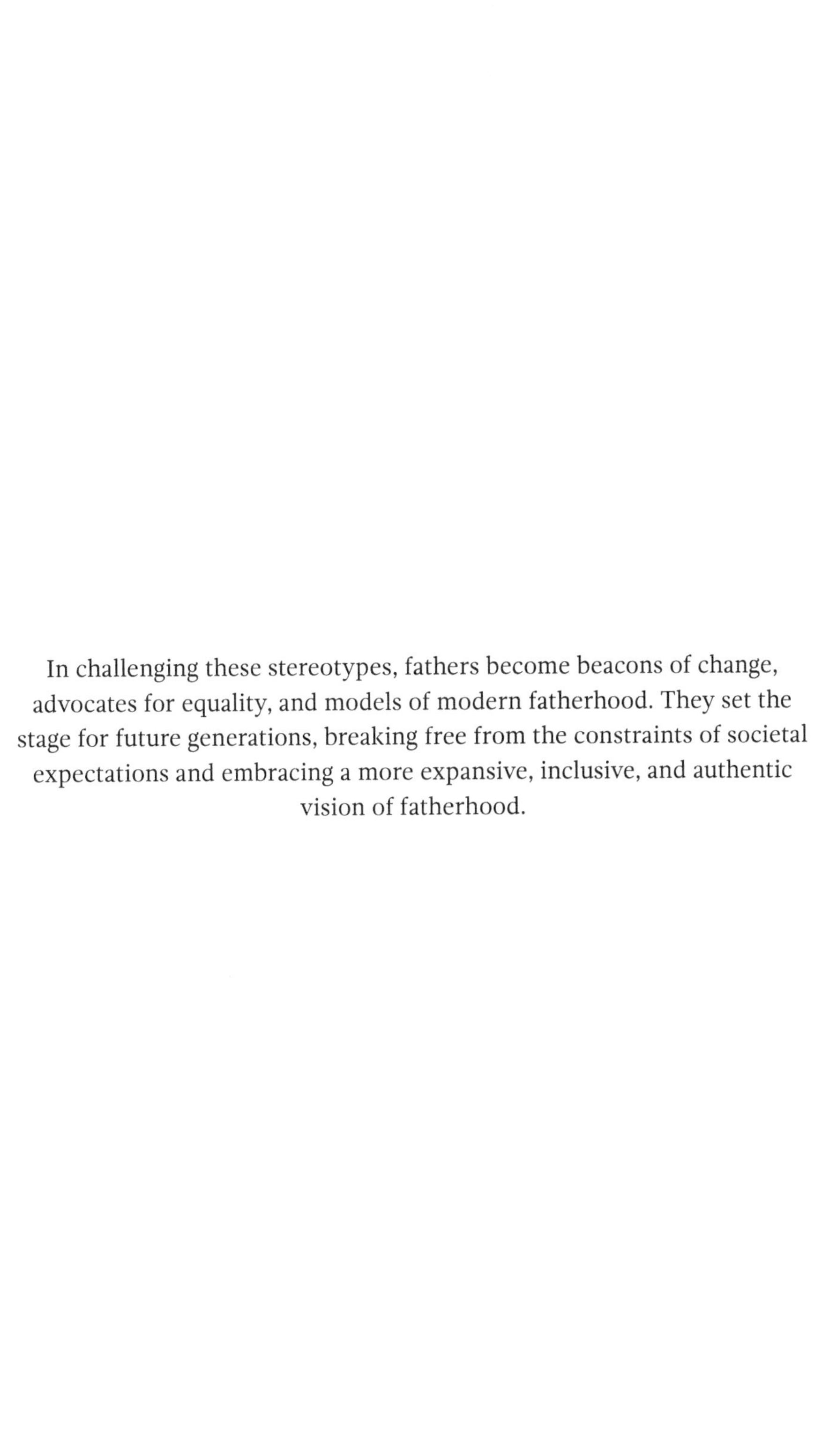

In challenging these stereotypes, fathers become beacons of change, advocates for equality, and models of modern fatherhood. They set the stage for future generations, breaking free from the constraints of societal expectations and embracing a more expansive, inclusive, and authentic vision of fatherhood.

His Loneliness

The loneliness of the father's journey is a poignant reality. While immersed in the duties and demands of raising a child, fathers often experience a profound sense of isolation. The weight of responsibility and societal expectations can create a barrier, making it challenging to connect with others who truly understand their struggles.

In the depths of their hearts, fathers yearn for meaningful connections and a sense of camaraderie. They seek solace in knowing that they are not alone in their experiences and that their emotions are valid. However, societal norms often perpetuate the idea that fathers should bear their burdens silently, keeping their struggles hidden from the world.

This isolation can be further intensified by the lack of spaces and support systems specifically designed for fathers. Parenting groups and resources predominantly cater to mothers, leaving fathers feeling excluded and overlooked. As a result, fathers may internalise their challenges, silently navigating the complexities of fatherhood without an outlet for expression or guidance.

Recognizing the importance of connection and support, fathers yearn for spaces where they can share their joys, fears, and frustrations without judgement. They seek empathetic ears and open hearts, understanding that vulnerability is not a sign of weakness but a pathway to growth and understanding. Through shared experiences, fathers can find solace in knowing that their struggles are universal and that their emotions are valid.

Open communication, empathy, and shared responsibilities create a network of support that can ease the loneliness and strengthen the bonds of fatherhood.

It is essential for society as a whole to recognize and address the loneliness experienced by fathers. By creating inclusive spaces that acknowledge and validate their experiences, we can dismantle the barriers that isolate fathers and promote a culture of support, understanding, and empathy.

Let us strive to create a world where fathers are encouraged to seek connection and support, where their voices are heard, and where their experiences are valued. Together, we can cultivate a community that uplifts fathers, providing them with the connection and support they need to thrive on their journey of fatherhood.

Embracing emotional Resilience

Emotional resilience is not about suppressing or denying emotions, but rather about acknowledging them, understanding their origins, and finding healthy ways to process and express them. It is a journey that requires self-reflection, self-compassion, and a willingness to confront vulnerabilities head-on.

In the solitude of quiet moments, fathers may find themselves grappling with a myriad of emotions—a cocktail of joy, fear, frustration, and love. They may question their abilities, worry about making mistakes, or feel overwhelmed by the weight of responsibility. But within these depths, there exists an opportunity for profound growth.

Through self-reflection, fathers can explore the origins of their emotions and uncover patterns that influence their responses. They can engage in introspective practices such as journaling, meditation, or seeking therapy, allowing them to gain insight into their inner world and develop a deeper understanding of themselves.

Self-compassion becomes a guiding light on this journey. Fathers must learn to embrace their imperfections, forgive themselves for their mistakes, and offer kindness and understanding to their own hearts. By cultivating self-compassion, they create a nurturing space for healing and growth, allowing themselves to learn and evolve as fathers and individuals.

Connecting with others who share similar experiences can also foster emotional resilience. Fathers can seek out support groups, online communities, or trusted confidants who offer empathy and understanding. Sharing stories, exchanging advice, and receiving validation from others who have walked a similar path can be immensely healing, reminding fathers that they are not alone in their struggles.

Embracing emotional resilience is an ongoing process. Fathers may encounter setbacks and face new challenges along the way. However, by nurturing a sense of self-awareness and self-care, fathers develop the tools to navigate the emotional landscape of fatherhood with grace and authenticity.

CHAPTER TWO

SACRIFICES AND PRIORITIES

In this deeply moving chapter, 'The Father' delves into the profound sacrifices and unwavering dedication that fathers demonstrate in their roles. It explores the choices and trade-offs they make, often putting their own needs and desires aside to prioritize the well-being and happiness of their children and families. The chapter highlights the countless sacrifices fathers willingly undertake, from long hours at work to missed opportunities and personal ambitions, all in the name of providing a better life for their loved ones. Through heartfelt stories and reflections, readers gain a profound appreciation for the selflessness and unconditional love that fathers embody. The chapter serves as a tribute to their unwavering commitment and sheds light on the challenges and rewards of balancing personal aspirations with the responsibilities of fatherhood. It invites readers to reflect on the sacrifices made by their own fathers or father figures, fostering a greater understanding and appreciation for the sacrifices that shape their lives.

Unveiling Sacrifices

Within the depths of fatherhood's embrace, lies a sacred journey of sacrifices, each one etched upon the heart with profound emotional resonance. These sacrifices, often unseen and unspoken, deserve to be unveiled and honoured, offering a closer look into the intricate landscape of the father's experience.

The sacrifices of a father encompass a myriad of emotions, from the joyous surrender of personal ambitions to the quiet moments of selflessness that shape the very essence of his being. They are the tender whispers of affection, the soothing presence during sleepless nights, and the unwavering dedication to providing a stable and nurturing environment.

At the heart of these sacrifices lies the willingness to set aside one's own needs and desires, to put the needs of their children and family first. It is a selfless act of love, a testament to the depth of their commitment and the unyielding strength of their character.

In the realm of emotions, fathers may sacrifice their own vulnerability, shielding their loved ones from worry or distress. They carry the weight of their own fears and anxieties, shouldering the burdens of their family with steadfast resolve. The silent battles fought within their hearts go unnoticed, yet they shape the very essence of their journey.

The sacrifices of a father also extend to the realm of time and presence. They willingly give up personal pursuits and moments of solitude to be present for their children's milestones, to offer guidance, and to be a source of unwavering support. They may trade in their own leisure and hobbies for bedtime stories, backyard adventures, and cherished family traditions.

Financial sacrifices, too, mark the path of fatherhood. Fathers work tirelessly, sometimes at the cost of their own dreams, to ensure the well-being and future of their loved ones. They make choices that prioritise the needs of their family, sacrificing immediate gratification for long-term stability and security.

In the curtain of sacrifice, fathers embody strength and resilience. They weather storms, overcome obstacles, and make difficult choices with grace and determination. Their sacrifices may go unnoticed by the world, but they form the foundation of a loving and nurturing home, shaping the lives of their children and generations to come.

The Tug Of Priorities

In the labyrinth of fatherhood, there exists an eternal tug of priorities—a constant balancing act between various aspects of life. The responsibilities of being a father often collide with career aspirations, personal desires, and the needs of others. Navigating this delicate balance requires careful consideration and a deep understanding of one's values and commitments.

At the heart of this struggle lies the challenge of allocating time and attention. Fathers find themselves torn between dedicating quality moments to their children and fulfilling their obligations in other areas of life. The desire to be fully present for their children's milestones and daily needs competes with work demands, household responsibilities, and personal interests.

Prioritising family means making conscious choices to invest time and energy into nurturing the bond with their children. It means being present during important events, actively engaging in their development, and creating a loving and supportive environment. It requires recognizing that these moments are fleeting and that the investment made in the early years lays the foundation for a lifetime of connection.

However, the tug of priorities also extends beyond the realm of parenting. Fathers grapple with the desire to pursue their own dreams and ambitions while fulfilling their role as a caregiver. They may face difficult decisions, sacrificing personal aspirations for the sake of their family's well-being. It is a delicate dance of finding harmony between personal fulfilment and the sacrifices required for their loved ones.

The external pressures of society and societal expectations can further complicate the tug of priorities. Fathers may feel the weight of traditional gender roles, where the sole provider role clashes with the desire for more involvement in their children's lives. Challenging these stereotypes requires courage and a willingness to forge a path that aligns with one's own values and the unique dynamics of their family.

Finding equilibrium in the midst of competing priorities is an ongoing journey. It requires open communication, flexibility, and a willingness to adapt to changing circumstances. Fathers must continually assess their values and commitments, making conscious choices that align with their vision of a fulfilling and balanced life.

In the tug of priorities, fathers discover the power of intentionality. They learn to make mindful decisions that honour their values and the needs of their loved ones. It is a dance of give and take, a delicate balancing act that requires constant recalibration.

May fathers navigate the complexities of the tug of priorities with grace and wisdom. May they find solace in knowing that their choices are driven by love and a deep commitment to their family. And may they discover a sense of fulfilment in the beautiful tapestry of fatherhood, where the tug of priorities weaves a story of devotion, growth, and profound connection.

Time Sacrifice

Time, the elusive currency of life, becomes a sacrificial gift in the realm of fatherhood. As fathers travel on their journey, they are confronted with the delicate task of balancing the limited resource of time between various demands and responsibilities.

Every moment spent with their children holds immeasurable value, as time has a way of slipping through their fingers like grains of sand. Fathers recognize the fleeting nature of childhood and the importance of creating lasting memories and meaningful connections.

Sacrificing time for the sake of their children means consciously choosing presence over absence. It involves being there for the milestones, the bedtime stories, the playtime in the park, and the conversations that shape their children's world. It means setting aside personal pursuits and distractions to invest undivided attention in the precious moments that build the foundation of their relationship.

In the face of demanding careers, household responsibilities, and personal obligations, fathers make sacrifices to ensure that their children receive the gift of their time. They may trade leisurely pursuits for bedtime rituals, sacrifice moments of solitude for family outings, and adjust their schedules to be present for important events in their children's lives.

Sacrificing time also means finding a delicate balance between work and family. Fathers strive to provide financial security and stability for their loved ones, but they recognize that true wealth lies in the richness of shared experiences and quality time spent together. They make conscious choices to allocate their time in a way that aligns with their values and priorities, fostering a sense of connection and nurturing the bonds that strengthen their family unit.

Amidst the sacrifices, fathers come to understand that time is a finite resource, and its allocation requires mindful consideration. They learn to say no to distractions and commitments that hinder their ability to be fully present for their children. They may rearrange schedules, make sacrifices in their personal lives, and embrace the art of time management to create the space needed to prioritise their children.

In this sacrificial dance with time, fathers discover the immeasurable rewards that it brings. They witness the growth and development of their children, cherishing the milestones, the laughter, and the tender moments that shape their journey together. They find solace in knowing that their sacrifices have contributed to the well-being and happiness of their loved ones.

May fathers embrace the sacrificial gift of time with open hearts and open arms. May they recognize its fleeting nature and make intentional choices that prioritise their children's well-being and nurture the bonds that endure. And may they find fulfilment in the precious moments they create, knowing that their sacrifices have woven a tapestry of love and connection that will forever be cherished.

Sacrifice as Currency

In the realm of fatherhood, sacrifice becomes a currency through which love and devotion are expressed. Fathers willingly offer parts of themselves, making selfless choices that shape the lives of their children and families.

Financial sacrifice holds a significant place within this currency. Fathers understand the responsibility of providing for their loved ones, often working tirelessly to meet the material needs of their family. They may make sacrifices in their own desires and aspirations, redirecting resources towards the well-being and future of their children. This could mean forgoing personal luxuries, delaying career advancements, or making budgetary adjustments to ensure stability and security.

Beyond monetary sacrifices, fathers also give of their time and energy. They invest countless hours in their children's upbringing, putting their own needs aside to be fully present. This may involve attending school events, extracurricular activities, and creating meaningful traditions that foster connection. They sacrifice personal leisure and moments of solitude to engage in the daily joys and challenges of parenting, actively participating in the growth and development of their children.

Emotional sacrifice forms an integral part of this currency as well. Fathers may suppress their own fears and worries, bearing the weight of their loved ones' struggles on their shoulders. They provide a pillar of strength, offering unwavering support during difficult times. They sacrifice their own emotional well-being for the sake of their family, often putting on a brave face and offering a source of stability and comfort.

The currency of sacrifice is not without its challenges. Fathers may grapple with the internal struggle of balancing their own needs and desires with the responsibilities of fatherhood. They may experience moments of self-doubt, questioning if their sacrifices are enough or if they have made the right choices. However, their unwavering commitment to their family propels them forward, as they recognize that the sacrifices they make contribute to the greater good of their loved ones.

They witness the impact of their choices in the smiles, achievements, and growth of their children. They understand that the currency they offer holds immeasurable value, enriching the lives of those they hold dear.

May fathers continue to embrace the currency of sacrifice with compassion and grace. May they find strength in the knowledge that their sacrifices are an expression of love, shaping the lives of their children and families. And may they recognize that the greatest rewards lie not in the sacrifices themselves, but in the profound connections and lasting legacies they create through their selfless acts.

Sacrifice of Dreams

In the journey of fatherhood, there are moments when dreams take a backseat to the needs and responsibilities of family life. Fathers often find themselves making the difficult choice to defer their own aspirations in order to prioritise the well-being and happiness of their loved ones.

The path of fatherhood may intersect with personal dreams and ambitions, requiring fathers to reassess their priorities and make sacrifices. They may put aside career advancements, educational pursuits, or creative endeavours to create a stable and nurturing environment for their children. This act of selflessness allows them to redirect their energy and resources towards supporting their family's growth and providing a strong foundation for their children's future.

The decision to defer dreams is not always easy. Fathers may grapple with feelings of longing or a sense of unfulfilled potential. They may wonder about the possibilities that could have been if circumstances were different. Yet, they find solace in knowing that their sacrifices contribute to the happiness and success of their children.

Deferring dreams is not an act of resignation but rather a conscious choice rooted in love and devotion. Fathers recognize that their sacrifices are an investment in the lives of their children, nurturing their talents and providing them with opportunities for growth. They understand that the fulfilment they derive from witnessing their children's accomplishments and happiness outweighs any personal ambitions they may have set aside.

In this act of deferring dreams, fathers embody resilience and adaptability. They find new sources of fulfilment and purpose within the role of being a loving and supportive parent. They discover that the dreams they once had may transform or evolve as they embrace the joys and challenges of fatherhood.

While dreams may be deferred, they are not forgotten. Fathers may carry their aspirations within their hearts, finding ways to pursue them in smaller ways or later stages of life. They serve as role models to their children, demonstrating the importance of resilience, perseverance, and the pursuit of one's passions.

May fathers find solace in their choice to defer dreams. May they celebrate the achievements and dreams realised through their children's accomplishments. And may they find fulfilment in the knowledge that their sacrifices have played a vital role in shaping the lives and futures of their loved ones.

Shift in Priorities

The arrival of a child brings with it a reordering of priorities. Fathers recognize that their role as a caregiver and provider takes precedence over personal pursuits and desires. They willingly adjust their lives, redirecting their energy towards creating a nurturing and supportive environment for their family.

Career aspirations may take a backseat as fathers prioritise spending quality time with their children. They understand that these precious moments are fleeting and cannot be reclaimed. The once-ambitious pursuit of professional success now becomes intertwined with the desire to be present for their children's milestones, to witness their growth, and to forge deep connections that will last a lifetime.

In the realm of shifting priorities, fathers also become attuned to the needs and well-being of their partners. They recognize the importance of fostering a strong and loving relationship, nurturing a partnership that supports the growth and development of their children. They make deliberate choices to invest time and effort into maintaining a healthy balance between their roles as fathers, partners, and individuals.

The shift in priorities extends beyond the immediate family. Fathers become aware of their role in shaping the future of society and the world at large. They understand the importance of instilling values such as empathy, compassion, and integrity in their children, knowing that these qualities will have a far-reaching impact on the communities they will one day belong to.

While the shift in priorities can bring about challenges and sacrifices, fathers find deep fulfilment in aligning their lives with what truly matters. They witness the positive effects of their choices in the smiles, laughter, and growth of their children. They cherish the intimate moments, the shared experiences, and the profound connections that are nurtured as a result of their shifting priorities.

May fathers continue shifting priorities with wisdom and grace. May they find solace in knowing that their choices shape the lives of their loved ones and contribute to a more loving and compassionate world. And may they embrace this transformative journey with open hearts, recognizing the immeasurable value of aligning their actions with the well-being and happiness of their family.

How to create a balance ?

In the symphony of fatherhood, there exists a delicate dance between the self and the family—a sacred balance that fathers strive to achieve. They navigate the intricate dynamics of their own needs, aspirations, and growth, while simultaneously tending to the needs of their loved ones.

Within the sacred balance, fathers seek opportunities for personal growth and fulfilment. They pursue their passions, hobbies, and interests, recognizing that their own sense of purpose and fulfilment positively impacts the atmosphere within their family. They honour their individuality and strive to maintain a sense of identity outside of their role as a father, allowing their unique qualities and talents to shine.

At the same time, fathers embrace the profound responsibility of nurturing their family. They devote time, energy, and resources to creating a safe and loving environment where their children can thrive. They engage in meaningful conversations, provide guidance, and offer unwavering support, fostering a sense of belonging and empowerment within their family unit.

The sacred balance involves setting boundaries and making choices that honour both the self and the family. Fathers learn to prioritise their time and commitments, ensuring they have the space to fulfil their own needs while being present for their loved ones. They cultivate open communication within the family, fostering an atmosphere of understanding and mutual respect.

The interplay of self and family in the sacred balance also extends to the development of relationships outside the immediate family unit. Fathers recognize the importance of fostering connections with extended family, friends, and communities. They understand that these relationships enrich their lives and provide a support system that strengthens the well-being of their family as a whole.

They navigate the ebb and flow of their own growth and the needs of their family, making choices that honour the sacred bond between self and loved ones. They understand that in nurturing themselves, they create a ripple effect of love, support, and resilience that permeates their family and beyond.

CHAPTER THREE

THE FATHER AS ROLE MODEL

In this powerful chapter, 'The Father' explores the significant role fathers play as influential role models in the lives of their children. It delves into the profound impact that fathers have on shaping their children's values, beliefs, and behaviors through their words, actions, and presence. The chapter emphasizes the importance of positive male role models in a child's development, highlighting the ways in which fathers inspire, guide, and instill important life lessons. It delves into the qualities and characteristics that fathers embody as role models, such as strength, integrity, compassion, and perseverance. Through heartfelt stories and personal anecdotes, readers gain insight into the transformative influence fathers have on their children's lives and the lasting legacy they leave behind. The chapter encourages readers to reflect on the role models they had in their own lives and the ways in which their fathers or father figures have shaped their own journeys. It inspires readers to embrace their roles as fathers and strive to be positive and empowering influences in the lives of their children, leaving a powerful and lasting impact on their growth and development.

Fathers as Moral Guides

In fatherhood, fathers serve as beacons of morality, leading their children by example and instilling in them the values that shape their character. Through their actions, fathers demonstrate integrity, compassion, and strength, leaving an indelible imprint on their children's lives.

With unwavering conviction, fathers uphold a code of ethics that guides their interactions with the world. They embody honesty, showing their children the power of truth, even in the face of adversity. They teach accountability, taking responsibility for their actions and demonstrating the importance of integrity in all endeavours.

Fathers radiate kindness and empathy, leaving a trail of compassion wherever they go. They extend a helping hand to those in need, teaching their children the value of lending support and understanding to others. Through their acts of kindness, fathers inspire their children to embrace empathy as a cornerstone of their own character.

In the realm of strength, fathers redefine traditional notions by embracing vulnerability. They demonstrate the courage to express their emotions, teaching their children that strength lies not in suppressing feelings, but in acknowledging and embracing them. By doing so, fathers create an environment where emotions are celebrated, nurturing emotional intelligence and resilience in their children.

Fathers understand the weight of their influence and take deliberate steps to foster positive behaviours and attitudes. They model patience, teaching their children the virtue of perseverance and the rewards that come with it. They exhibit respect, treating others with dignity and encouraging their children to do the same. Through their actions, fathers cultivate an environment where kindness, respect, and perseverance flourish.

With every interaction, fathers teach their children the power of empathy and understanding. They encourage their children to walk in the shoes of others, to consider diverse perspectives, and to practise compassion in their relationships. By fostering empathy, fathers equip their children with a profound sense of connection and a genuine desire to make the world a better place.

In the journey of fatherhood, fathers are not only teachers but perpetual students of life. They engage in self-reflection, acknowledging their own imperfections, and actively striving for personal growth. By demonstrating this commitment to self-improvement, fathers show their children the transformative power of continuous learning and the importance of embracing challenges as opportunities for growth.

Through their unwavering support, fathers create a foundation for their children to thrive and blossom. They encourage independence, providing guidance and a safety net as their children navigate their own paths. Fathers celebrate their children's achievements, no matter how big or small, fostering a sense of confidence and self-belief that fuels their children's pursuit of their dreams.

With each step on this journey, fathers leave an enduring legacy. Through their unwavering commitment to leading by example, fathers shape the next generation, nurturing compassionate and ethical leaders who will carry forward the values they have instilled. In their embrace of vulnerability, their embodiment of empathy, and their commitment to personal growth, fathers create a ripple effect of positive change that reaches far beyond the bounds of their own families.

May fathers continue to illuminate the path of morality, leading their children with unwavering strength and boundless love. May they inspire generations to come with their affirmative actions and shape a future built on integrity, compassion, and unwavering principles.

Accept Vulnerability

In the travel of fatherhood, there exists a transformative power in embracing vulnerability. Fathers, with courageous hearts, shatter the barriers that separate them from their children, creating a space of authentic connection and emotional growth.

Traditionally, fathers have been encouraged to embody strength and stoicism, to suppress their vulnerabilities for the sake of societal expectations. However, enlightened fathers understand that true strength lies in vulnerability, in allowing themselves to be seen and felt by their children.

With open hearts, fathers create a safe haven where emotions are acknowledged and expressed without judgement. They show their children that it is okay to feel deeply, to experience a full range of emotions, and to navigate the complexities of life with grace and vulnerability.

Through vulnerability, fathers dismantle the walls that hinder deep connections. They share their stories, their triumphs, and their struggles, creating a bridge of understanding between generations. In doing so, fathers invite their children to share their own vulnerabilities, fostering an environment of trust, empathy, and emotional intimacy.

In this sacred space of vulnerability, fathers encourage their children to embrace their true selves. They affirm their children's uniqueness and celebrate their individuality, instilling in them a sense of self-acceptance and confidence. By showing vulnerability, fathers teach their children that it is through embracing their authentic selves that they can truly thrive.

Vulnerability also empowers fathers to address their own wounds and insecurities. They acknowledge their imperfections, learn from their mistakes, and embark on a journey of self-discovery and healing. In doing so, fathers model resilience and growth, inspiring their children to navigate their own challenges with courage and vulnerability.

By embracing vulnerability, fathers demonstrate that it is not weakness, but rather a strength of character. They teach their children that vulnerability is the gateway to deep connection, empathy, and genuine relationships. They encourage their children to extend compassion and understanding to others, recognizing that vulnerability is a universal human experience.

In the dance of vulnerability, fathers inspire their children to embrace their emotions, to find strength in vulnerability, and to be agents of change in a world that often values walls over bridges. They set a powerful example, showing their children that vulnerability is an essential ingredient in living a fulfilling and meaningful life.

As fathers embrace vulnerability, they embark on a transformative journey that transcends generations. They create a legacy of emotional openness and authentic connection, leaving an imprint on their children that extends far beyond their years together. Many fathers continue to lead the way, fearlessly embracing vulnerability and empowering their children to do the same. May they nurture a world where vulnerability is celebrated, and where genuine connections flourish.

Training his child the Life Skills

Fathers hold the key to equipping their children with practical life skills that will guide them on their journey towards success. As teachers, fathers provide invaluable lessons that extend far beyond the classroom, nurturing their children's abilities to navigate the complexities of life.

Problem-solving is a fundamental skill fathers instil in their children. They encourage their children to approach challenges with a curious and analytical mindset, helping them develop creative solutions and think critically. By fostering problem-solving skills, fathers empower their children to face obstacles head-on and overcome them with confidence.

Effective communication is another vital skill fathers teach their children. They model clear and respectful communication, emphasising active listening and the power of expressing oneself articulately. Through open and honest conversations, fathers encourage their children to find their voice and communicate their thoughts, feelings, and ideas effectively.

Resilience is a life skill fathers cultivate within their children. They teach their children to persevere in the face of adversity, to bounce back from failures, and to learn from setbacks. By imparting resilience, fathers equip their children with the strength and determination needed to weather life's storms and emerge stronger.

Self-discipline is a cornerstone of success, and fathers play a crucial role in nurturing this skill. They instil in their children the importance of setting goals, managing their time effectively, and staying focused on their priorities. Through consistent guidance and setting high expectations, fathers help their children develop self-discipline and a strong work ethic.

Financial literacy is an essential life skill that fathers impart to their children. They teach them the value of money, how to budget and save, and the importance of making sound financial decisions. Fathers empower their children to understand the principles of financial responsibility, enabling them to build a solid foundation for their future.

Decision-making is a skill fathers help their children develop. They encourage critical thinking, weighing the pros and cons of choices, and considering the potential consequences. By guiding their children through the decision-making process, fathers teach them how to make informed choices and take ownership of their actions.

Adaptability is a skill fathers foster in their children. They expose them to new experiences, encourage them to embrace change, and teach them to be flexible in the face of unexpected circumstances. Fathers equip their children with the ability to adapt to different situations, fostering resilience and the capacity to thrive in a rapidly evolving world.

These life skills are invaluable gifts that fathers bestow upon their children. By teaching problem-solving, communication, resilience, self-discipline, financial literacy, decision-making, and adaptability, fathers lay a strong foundation for their children's success and empower them to navigate life's challenges with confidence and competence.

Teaching Gender Equality

Fathers teach their children the importance of gender equality through their own actions and words. They model respectful and egalitarian relationships, treating all individuals with dignity and fairness, regardless of gender. Fathers encourage their children to challenge traditional gender stereotypes and embrace the diversity of identities and abilities that exist within our society.

Through open and honest conversations, fathers address topics related to gender equality. They discuss the importance of equal opportunities and rights for all, highlighting the need to challenge gender biases and discrimination. Fathers educate their children about the historical struggles for gender equality and inspire them to be agents of change in their own lives and communities.

Fathers foster empathy and compassion in their children, teaching them to value and appreciate the experiences and perspectives of others, regardless of gender. They encourage their children to listen attentively, to show understanding, and to support those who face gender-based challenges. By nurturing empathy, fathers cultivate a sense of responsibility towards creating a more just and equitable world.

In the realm of parenting, fathers share household responsibilities equally with their partners, demonstrating that caregiving and domestic tasks are not solely the domain of one gender. They actively participate in child-rearing activities, nurturing their children's emotional and physical well-being. Through their actions, fathers challenge traditional gender roles and foster an environment where all individuals, regardless of gender, can thrive.

Fathers promote education and opportunity for all their children, regardless of their gender. They encourage their daughters to pursue their dreams and aspirations, instilling in them a sense of confidence and empowerment. Fathers teach their sons to respect and value the contributions and achievements of women, inspiring them to become advocates for gender equality.

By nurturing gender equality, fathers equip their children with the tools to challenge discrimination and bias in all areas of life. They teach their children to be allies, to speak up against injustice, and to actively promote inclusivity. Fathers create a safe and supportive environment where their children can explore their own identities, free from societal pressures and expectations.

In this journey of nurturing gender equality, fathers contribute to building a more equitable and harmonious society. By instilling in their children a deep understanding of the value of all genders and the importance of equal rights and opportunities, fathers play a pivotal role in shaping a future where everyone is treated with dignity, respect, and fairness.

Cultivating Empathy

Fathers have a profound role in cultivating empathy within their children. By fostering a deep understanding and compassion for others, fathers shape their children's ability to connect, relate, and make a positive impact in the world.

Fathers lead by example, demonstrating empathy in their daily interactions. They show kindness and understanding towards others, modelling how to be attentive listeners and offering support without judgement. Through their actions, fathers teach their children the importance of considering the feelings and experiences of others.

Fathers create a safe and nurturing environment where empathy can thrive. They encourage their children to express their emotions and actively listen to the emotions of others. Fathers validate their children's feelings, teaching them that empathy begins with acknowledging and understanding one's own emotions.

Through storytelling and shared experiences, fathers expose their children to different perspectives and cultures. They encourage their children to step into the shoes of others, fostering empathy by broadening their understanding of diverse backgrounds and life experiences.

Fathers teach their children the value of empathy in resolving conflicts and fostering positive relationships. They guide their children in navigating disagreements with kindness and respect, encouraging them to consider the feelings and needs of others. Fathers empower their children to find common ground and seek win-win solutions.

By engaging in acts of service and giving back to the community, fathers instil a sense of empathy and compassion in their children. They involve their children in charitable activities, volunteer work, and acts of kindness, emphasising the importance of helping those in need. Fathers nurture a spirit of empathy by teaching their children to extend a helping hand to others.

Fathers encourage their children to practise empathy in the digital age. They teach them the importance of respectful communication online, discouraging cyberbullying and promoting empathy in their virtual interactions. Fathers guide their children in using technology responsibly and in fostering positive online communities.

Through their words and actions, fathers emphasise the significance of empathy in creating a more inclusive and compassionate society. They inspire their children to stand up against injustice, to show empathy towards marginalised groups, and to actively work towards a world where everyone is treated with dignity and fairness.

In the journey of cultivating empathy, fathers nurture their children's ability to connect deeply with others, to understand diverse perspectives, and to contribute to the well-being of their communities. By instilling empathy, fathers shape their children into compassionate individuals who will make a positive difference in the lives of others.

Encouraging Self-Reflection

Fathers play a crucial role in fostering self-reflection within their children by guiding them to look inward, fathers empower their children to develop self-awareness, explore their values, and cultivate personal growth.

Fathers create a space of introspection and self-reflection by encouraging their children to pause and contemplate their thoughts, feelings, and actions. They teach them the importance of taking time for self-reflection as a means of gaining insight into themselves and their experiences.

Through open and honest conversations, fathers prompt their children to reflect on their strengths, weaknesses, and areas for growth. They help them recognize their unique talents and abilities, fostering a sense of self-confidence and belief in their own potential.

Fathers challenge their children to examine their beliefs, values, and attitudes. They encourage critical thinking and help their children understand the impact of their choices and actions on themselves and others. By fostering self-reflection, fathers empower their children to align their behaviours with their values and make choices that are authentic to who they are.

In times of conflict or challenges, fathers guide their children to reflect on their role and responsibility in the situation. They teach them to assess their actions, consider alternative perspectives, and seek resolutions that promote understanding and growth. Through this process, fathers cultivate a sense of accountability and resilience within their children.

Fathers also encourage their children to reflect on their emotions, helping them understand the root causes and triggers of their feelings. They teach them to identify and manage their emotions in healthy ways, promoting emotional intelligence and well-being. Fathers create a supportive environment where their children can freely express and explore their emotions.

Through self-reflection, fathers help their children set and evaluate goals. They guide them in assessing their progress, identifying areas of improvement, and celebrating their achievements. Fathers instil a sense of purpose and motivation in their children, encouraging them to strive for personal growth and fulfilment.

Fathers model self-reflection by engaging in their own introspective practices. They openly share their own journeys of self-discovery and growth, inspiring their children to embark on their own paths of self-reflection. By leading by example, fathers demonstrate the ongoing nature of self-reflection and the importance of continual learning and development.

In the journey of encouraging self-reflection, fathers empower their children to navigate life with greater self-awareness and intention. By fostering introspection, fathers lay the foundation for their children to cultivate personal growth, make informed choices, and live a fulfilling and purposeful life.

Balancing Support and Independence

Fathers face the delicate task of striking a balance between providing support to their children and fostering their independence. This balance is crucial for their children's growth, self-discovery, and the development of their own strengths and abilities.

Fathers offer unwavering support to their children, creating a safe and nurturing environment where they can explore their passions and interests. They encourage their children to pursue their dreams, providing guidance and encouragement along the way. Fathers offer a listening ear, a shoulder to lean on, and a source of unwavering love and acceptance.

At the same time, fathers understand the importance of allowing their children to experience and learn from challenges. They foster independence by giving their children the space to make decisions and face the consequences of their choices. Fathers provide guidance and advice, but also encourage their children to take ownership of their actions and learn from both successes and failures.

Fathers strike a delicate balance between offering support and allowing their children to learn from their own experiences. They recognize that by allowing their children to face and overcome obstacles, they build resilience, self-confidence, and the ability to navigate life's challenges independently.

Fathers nurture their children's independence by encouraging them to explore their own interests, make their own decisions, and take responsibility for their actions. They provide guidance and mentorship, but ultimately trust their children to make choices that align with their values and aspirations.

Through open and honest communication, fathers create a safe space for their children to express their desires, dreams, and concerns. They actively listen to their children's thoughts and feelings, validating their experiences and offering guidance when needed. Fathers foster a sense of trust and open dialogue, which allows their children to seek support while also developing their own autonomy.

Fathers recognize that the journey towards independence is not a linear path, but rather a process of growth and self-discovery. They embrace the role of a supportive guide, offering a helping hand when their children need it, while also respecting their boundaries and allowing them to explore their own capabilities.

In the journey of balancing support and independence, fathers provide a solid foundation of love, support, and guidance, while also empowering their children to become self-reliant, confident individuals. By striking this delicate balance, fathers equip their children with the tools and mindset to navigate life with resilience, independence, and a strong sense of self.

Implementing Diversity

Fathers play a crucial role in celebrating diversity and promoting inclusivity within their children's lives.Fathers teach their children to respect and honour the diversity that exists in the world. They encourage their children to be curious and open-minded, seeking to learn about different cultures, traditions, and perspectives. Fathers foster a sense of cultural sensitivity, guiding their children to embrace diversity as an opportunity for growth and understanding.

By exposing their children to diverse experiences, fathers broaden their horizons and challenge stereotypes and biases. They encourage their children to engage with individuals from different backgrounds, fostering friendships that transcend differences and promote mutual respect and empathy.

Fathers educate their children about the importance of equal rights and social justice. They empower their children to stand up against discrimination and advocate for inclusivity and fairness. Fathers teach their children that embracing diversity is not only a moral responsibility, but also an enriching and fulfilling way to engage with the world.

Through storytelling and literature, fathers introduce their children to diverse narratives and perspectives. They share stories that reflect the experiences of people from various backgrounds, teaching their children about the challenges they may face and the triumphs they achieve. Fathers inspire their children to be allies and advocates for those who face prejudice and discrimination.

Fathers celebrate diversity within their own families, fostering an environment where all family members feel valued and respected. They honour and appreciate the unique strengths and talents that each individual brings, creating a sense of belonging and unity. Fathers encourage their children to express their own identities authentically, embracing their cultural heritage and individual differences.

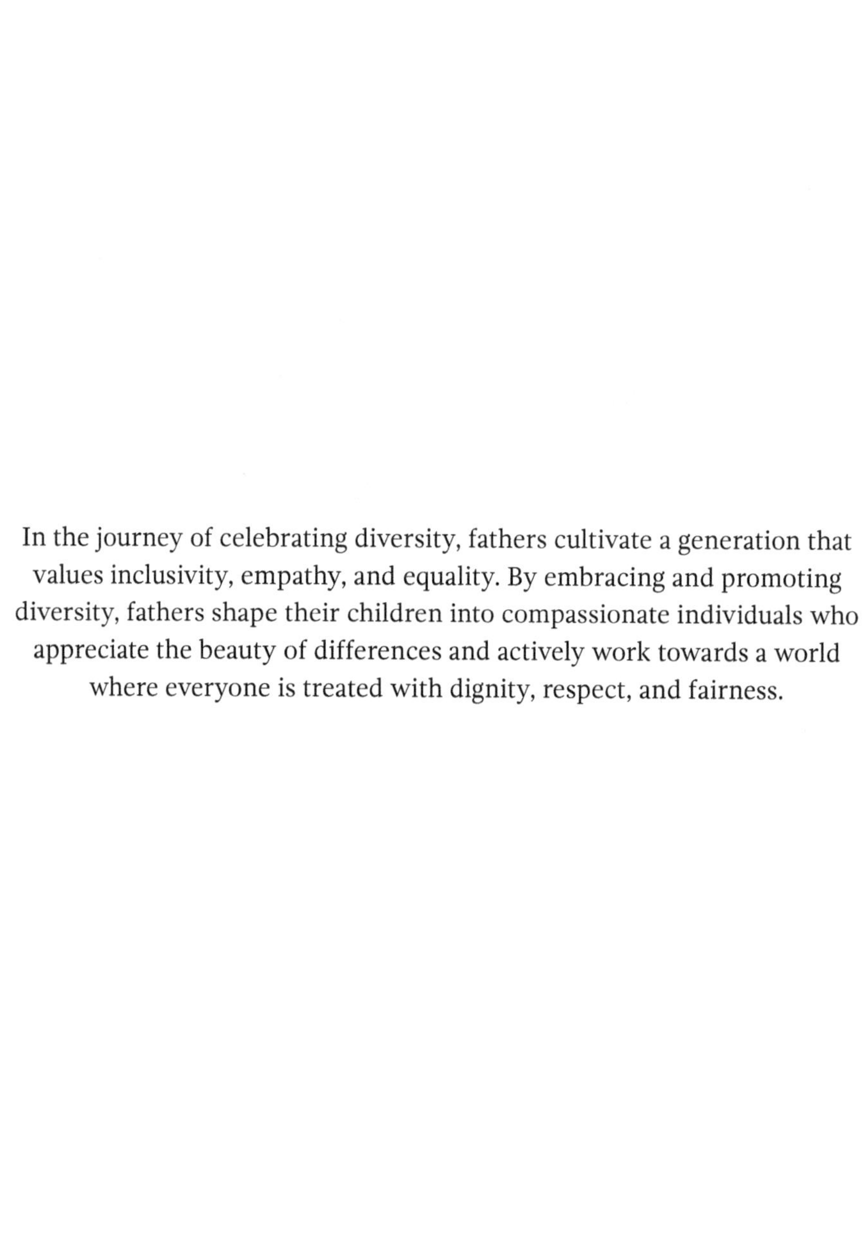

In the journey of celebrating diversity, fathers cultivate a generation that values inclusivity, empathy, and equality. By embracing and promoting diversity, fathers shape their children into compassionate individuals who appreciate the beauty of differences and actively work towards a world where everyone is treated with dignity, respect, and fairness.

CHAPTER FOUR

Overcoming Societal Expectations

In this thought-provoking chapter, 'The Father' delves into the challenges and pressures fathers face due to societal expectations and norms. It explores the narrow definitions of fatherhood imposed by society and the impact it can have on fathers' self-perception, relationships, and overall well-being. The chapter sheds light on the importance of breaking free from these expectations and embracing a more authentic and fulfilling version of fatherhood.

Through personal anecdotes and insightful narratives, the chapter highlights the struggles fathers encounter in trying to live up to societal ideals and the internal conflicts they may experience. It delves into the emotional journey of fathers as they navigate the expectations of being strong, stoic providers, while also longing for emotional connection and active involvement in their children's lives.

Moreover, the chapter provides empowering solutions and strategies for overcoming societal expectations. It encourages fathers to challenge traditional gender roles and stereotypes, fostering an environment that values emotional expression, nurturing, and shared parenting responsibilities. It emphasizes the importance of self-acceptance, self-compassion, and finding a balance between fulfilling societal roles and embracing personal values and aspirations.

By unpacking the societal pressures placed on fathers, this chapter aims to inspire readers to redefine fatherhood on their own terms and forge a path that aligns with their authentic selves. It encourages fathers to embrace their unique strengths, passions, and parenting styles, fostering meaningful connections with their children and creating a nurturing and supportive environment for their families. Ultimately, the chapter seeks to empower fathers to break free from societal constraints and find fulfillment and joy in their role as fathers, defying societal expectations with confidence and resilience.

Challenging Stereotypes of Fatherhood

In a world filled with preconceived notions and expectations, fatherhood often carries a set of stereotypes and prescribed roles. However, it is essential to challenge these societal expectations and break free from the mould to embrace a more authentic and fulfilling experience of fatherhood.

Many fathers find themselves navigating a narrow path defined by traditional gender roles, which can limit their expression and involvement in parenting. By acknowledging these limitations, we open up opportunities to redefine fatherhood and create a more inclusive and diverse understanding of what it means to be a father.

This section delves into the prevalent stereotypes placed on fathers and explores the pressures they can create. We examine the expectations that fathers should be stoic, the sole provider, or detached from the emotional aspects of parenting. By recognizing these stereotypes, fathers can begin the process of challenging them and forging their own unique path.

Challenging stereotypes of fatherhood can indeed be a complex and multifaceted journey. Here, let's explore some of the challenges that arise when defying stereotypes and provide solutions and illustrations to navigate them:

1. Societal Expectations:

Society often imposes rigid expectations on fathers, defining their roles primarily as providers and disciplinarians. When fathers deviate from these norms, they may face resistance and judgement.

Solution: To challenge these stereotypes, fathers can actively engage in open conversations with their families, friends, and communities, highlighting the importance of diverse and inclusive fatherhood roles. By sharing their personal stories and experiences, they can help broaden societal perceptions and promote acceptance of different parenting styles.

Illustration: Mr Rahul, a father who defies traditional stereotypes, faces scepticism from his own parents about his decision to take an extended parental leave to care for his newborn. However, by openly discussing his motivations, sharing his research on the benefits of paternal involvement, and demonstrating his commitment to nurturing his child, he gradually wins over their support and understanding.

2. Personal Identity:

Challenging stereotypes may require fathers to confront their own preconceived notions of masculinity and reconcile them with their desire to embrace a more diverse and inclusive version of fatherhood.

Solution: Fathers can engage in self-reflection and actively question societal norms and expectations. By redefining their own sense of masculinity and embracing a broader range of qualities, such as empathy, vulnerability, and emotional openness, they can create a positive impact on their own well-being and their children's development.

Illustration: Mr Mohan, a father who initially struggled with the notion of expressing emotions, gradually learns to challenge societal expectations. He engages in activities like journaling, therapy, and joining support groups that encourage self-reflection and emotional growth. As he becomes more comfortable with vulnerability, he models emotional authenticity for his children and fosters a more empathetic and understanding family dynamic.

3. Parental Bias:

Challenging stereotypes of fatherhood may involve confronting biases and assumptions within the parenting community, educational institutions, and even within oneself.

Solution: Fathers can actively seek out inclusive parenting communities and support networks where they can share experiences, seek guidance, and find affirmation. By actively participating in discussions and events that promote diverse perspectives, fathers can help break down barriers and challenge biases within these spaces.

Illustration: Daniel, a single father in a parenting group, encounters dismissive attitudes and assumptions about his ability to meet the emotional needs of his children. He responds by organising a session on the importance of involved fatherhood and invites guest speakers who share empowering stories. Through this initiative, he challenges parental biases and fosters a more inclusive environment within the group.

4. Work-Life Balance:

Challenging stereotypes may require fathers to navigate the delicate balance between work responsibilities and their involvement in caregiving.

Solution: Fathers can advocate for flexible work arrangements, engage in open communication with their employers, and set clear boundaries to prioritise their family commitments. By demonstrating their dedication to both their career and family, they challenge the notion that fathers must prioritise work above all else.

Illustration: Mr Krishna, a working father, negotiates with his employer for a flexible schedule that allows him to actively participate in his child's school activities. By showing the positive impact of his involvement on his productivity and job satisfaction, he challenges the stereotype that fathers who prioritise family are less committed to their careers.

By understanding and addressing these challenges head-on, fathers can navigate the process of challenging stereotypes of fatherhood with resilience and determination. Through their actions and personal growth, they contribute to the broader movement of redefining fatherhood, creating a more inclusive and accepting society for themselves and future generations.

Redefining Masculinity

In this section, we delve into the traditional notions of masculinity and their influence on fatherhood. We critically examine the limitations and challenges that arise from societal expectations of male behaviour, particularly in the context of parenting.

Toxic masculinity, with its rigid ideals and emphasis on dominance, can have a detrimental impact on father-child relationships. We explore the negative consequences of these societal pressures and encourage fathers to challenge and redefine traditional notions of masculinity.

A more inclusive and expansive definition of masculinity is promoted, one that embraces qualities such as emotional vulnerability, empathy, and nurturing. We highlight the importance of fathers embracing these traits as they navigate the journey of fatherhood.

Breaking free from gender stereotypes is essential in creating a nurturing and equal environment for both fathers and children. We discuss the benefits of fathers being actively involved in caregiving and nurturing activities, emphasising the positive impact it has on the well-being and development of children.

Shared parenting and equal partnership in raising children are explored as alternatives to traditional gender roles. By challenging the notion that caregiving is solely the responsibility of mothers, fathers can actively contribute to the upbringing of their children and foster a more balanced and harmonious family dynamic.

Practical strategies and resources are provided to support fathers in navigating and challenging traditional gender norms. By equipping fathers with tools to confront societal expectations, we empower them to be authentic and compassionate role models for their children.

Redefining masculinity and expanding the boundaries of fatherhood is a crucial step towards creating a more inclusive and equitable society. However, this process can be challenging due to various factors. Let's delve into some of these challenges and provide solutions and illustrations to navigate them:

1. Societal Expectations and Stereotypes:

Traditional notions of masculinity often limit the roles and expressions available to fathers, reinforcing expectations of stoicism, dominance, and traditional gender roles.

Solution: Fathers can challenge societal expectations by actively engaging in conversations and advocating for diverse representations of fatherhood. By sharing their experiences, expressing their emotions, and embracing a broader range of qualities associated with fatherhood, they can contribute to the redefinition of masculinity.

Illustration: Robert, a father who believes in nurturing his children's emotional well-being, faces criticism from relatives who consider his caring and nurturing approach as "unmanly." Robert responds by calmly explaining the importance of emotional connection and support in fostering his children's development. Over time, his relatives begin to appreciate and respect his parenting style, challenging their own biases about masculinity.

2. Personal Identity and Self-Reflection:

Redefining masculinity requires fathers to reflect on their own beliefs, biases, and conditioning about gender roles and challenge any internalised stereotypes.

Solution: Fathers can engage in self-reflection, education, and dialogue to unlearn societal norms and expand their understanding of masculinity. By embracing vulnerability, empathy, and emotional openness, fathers can redefine their own sense of self and fatherhood.

Illustration: James, a father who grew up in a household with rigid gender roles, embarks on a journey of self-discovery. He attends workshops, reads books, and engages in conversations about gender and masculinity.

Through this process, James becomes aware of the limitations he inherited and actively works to redefine his own masculinity, allowing him to foster a nurturing and egalitarian environment for his children.

3. Peer Pressure and Judgment:

Challenging traditional masculinity norms can subject fathers to peer pressure and judgement from others who may hold more rigid views.

Solution: Fathers can seek support from like-minded individuals and communities that value and encourage diverse expressions of fatherhood. By surrounding themselves with a supportive network, fathers can find the strength and affirmation to challenge societal pressures and stereotypes.

Illustration: Mr Ram, a father involved in his children's extracurricular activities, faces mockery from other fathers who adhere to traditional gender roles. Mr Ram finds solace in a local fathers' support group where he connects with other fathers who share similar values and experiences. Through this community, Mr Ram gains the confidence to continue being actively involved in his children's lives, despite societal pressures.

4. Balancing Work and Family Life:

Redefining masculinity in fatherhood often requires navigating the expectations and demands of the workplace while prioritising family commitments.

Solution: Fathers can advocate for family-friendly policies and work-life balance initiatives within their workplaces. By setting boundaries, communicating openly with employers, and seeking support from partners and co-workers, fathers can actively participate in their children's lives without compromising their careers.

Illustration: Thomas, a working father, negotiates a flexible work schedule that allows him to be present for important family moments. Initially met with resistance, Thomas provides his employer with evidence of the positive impact that work-life balance has on employee satisfaction and productivity. His employer, recognizing the value of supporting fathers, eventually agrees to the arrangement.

By acknowledging and addressing these challenges, fathers can play an active role in redefining masculinity and expanding the boundaries of fatherhood. Through their actions and perseverance, they contribute to a more inclusive and compassionate society, creating a healthier and more fulfilling environment for themselves, their children, and future generations.

Balancing Work and Family: Nurturing Both Spheres

In this section, we delve into the challenges of balancing work responsibilities with family commitments that fathers often face. We recognize the impact of work-life imbalance on fathers, children, and the overall well-being of the family.

We discuss strategies for setting priorities and managing time effectively, considering the unique demands and expectations that fathers encounter. Open communication with employers, colleagues, and family members is emphasised as a key aspect of achieving a harmonious balance.

Exploring flexible work arrangements and options for better work-life balance, we encourage fathers to seek out opportunities that allow them to actively participate in their children's lives. We provide practical tips for effective delegation and time management techniques to maximise efficiency and productivity in both spheres.

The importance of parental leave is discussed, advocating for its significance in allowing fathers to bond with their children and actively engage in caregiving responsibilities. We address the guilt and societal expectations that may surround fathers' involvement in family duties, emphasising the value of their presence and contribution.

Support networks and community resources play a vital role in navigating the challenges of balancing work and family. We explore the importance of seeking assistance from family, friends, and available support systems to alleviate the burden and create a more sustainable equilibrium.

We emphasise the significance of self-care and maintaining personal well-being amidst the demands of work and family. Setting boundaries and managing expectations, both at work and at home, is essential in preserving one's mental, emotional, and physical health.

Creating a supportive and inclusive work environment for fathers is crucial. We discuss the benefits of organisations fostering an atmosphere that recognizes and accommodates the needs of working fathers, promoting work-life integration and overall employee well-being.

Personal stories and experiences of fathers who have successfully achieved work-life balance are shared, providing inspiration and practical insights. Their journeys serve as a testament to the possibilities and rewards that come with nurturing both work and family domains.

Practical tips and resources are provided to support fathers in navigating the challenges of balancing work and family commitments. We equip them with the tools and knowledge needed to make informed decisions and prioritise their family's well-being.

Highlighting the long-term benefits of investing time and effort into both work and family, we emphasise the lasting impact of active fatherhood on the development and happiness of children. By prioritising family and striving for work-life balance, fathers can create a harmonious integration of their professional and personal lives.

Through this exploration of balancing work and family, we aim to inspire fathers to prioritise family time, nurture meaningful connections with their children, and create a fulfilling and harmonious life that encompasses both work and family.

Balancing work and family is an ongoing challenge for many fathers. The demands of work and the responsibilities of parenting can create conflicts and stress. Let's explore some of the challenges faced by fathers in balancing work and family, along with potential solutions and illustrations:

1. Long Working Hours and Career Expectations:

Many jobs demand long hours and may prioritise career advancement over family commitments, making it challenging for fathers to find a balance.

Solution: Fathers can communicate openly with their employers about their desire for work-life balance. Negotiating flexible work arrangements, such as adjusted schedules or remote work options, can help fathers better manage their time and fulfil their family responsibilities.

Illustration: Anupam, a dedicated father, speaks with his employer about the importance of family time. Recognizing his commitment and productivity, his employer agrees to a reduced work schedule that allows Anupam to spend more quality time with his children without compromising his career progress.

2. Guilt and Emotional Burden:

Fathers may experience guilt when they perceive their time away from family as a trade-off for their career, leading to emotional strain.

Solution: Fathers can prioritise self-care and seek support from their partners, friends, or support groups. Engaging in activities that promote well-being, such as exercise, hobbies, or meditation, can help fathers manage guilt and maintain their emotional well-being.

Illustration: Mr Krishna, a father struggling with guilt over spending less time with his children due to work commitments, starts attending a support group for working fathers. Through sharing experiences and receiving validation from other fathers, Mr Krishna gains a renewed sense of perspective and learns strategies to navigate guilt, allowing him to better balance his work and family life.

3. Limited Paternity Leave and Lack of Support:

In some countries and workplaces, paternity leave is limited, which can hinder fathers' ability to actively engage in early childcare responsibilities.

Solution: Fathers can advocate for extended paternity leave policies and seek support from organisations that promote work-life balance and fatherhood involvement. By encouraging conversations about the importance of paternity leave, fathers can drive change in policies and societal norms.

Illustration: Mr Mohan, a father passionate about supporting other fathers, joins an advocacy group that campaigns for extended paternity leave. Through their efforts, the group successfully lobbies for policy changes in their region, leading to increased paternity leave options for fathers, enabling them to spend more time bonding with their newborns.

4. Role Strain and Expectations:

Fathers may struggle with societal expectations that they solely provide for their family financially while also being actively involved in parenting.

Solution: Fathers can challenge traditional gender roles by sharing household responsibilities and parenting tasks with their partners. Open communication and negotiation within the family can help redefine expectations and create a more equitable division of labour.

Illustration: Mr Rahul and Lisa, a couple committed to shared responsibilities, have open discussions about their individual strengths and interests. They collaborate to create a system where household chores and parenting tasks are divided fairly, allowing both of them to balance their work and family responsibilities effectively.

5. Boundary Management:

Separating work and family time can be challenging, especially with technological advancements blurring the line between professional and personal life.

Solution: Fathers can establish clear boundaries by creating designated spaces for work and family activities. They can set aside dedicated time for family without interruptions from work-related tasks, fostering quality interactions with their children.

Illustration: Mr Emmanuvel, a father who works from home, creates a home office space where he can focus on work. He sets specific working hours and communicates with his family about the importance of uninterrupted work time. By doing so, he can be fully present and engaged with his children during non-working hours.

By recognizing and addressing these challenges, fathers can strive to find a better balance between work and family life.

Sharing Parenting: Partnering in Parenthood

In this chapter, we highlight the importance of shared parenting and the numerous benefits it brings to children and families. We discuss the shift away from traditional gender roles in parenting and the growing recognition of the value of equal partnership.

We explore the challenges and barriers faced in sharing parenting responsibilities, acknowledging the societal expectations and stereotypes that can hinder the progress towards equal co-parenting. Strategies for effective communication and decision-making as co-parents are provided, emphasising the importance of open and honest dialogue.

Creating a parenting plan and setting clear expectations and responsibilities are discussed as essential components of successful shared parenting. We delve into different parenting styles and the importance of finding common ground as co-parents, allowing for a cohesive approach to raising children.

The significance of teamwork and mutual support in parenting is emphasised. We provide practical tips for dividing household chores and child-rearing tasks equitably, promoting a shared sense of responsibility and ensuring that both parents are actively involved in all aspects of parenting.

We address the societal expectations and stereotypes surrounding parenting roles, encouraging fathers to play an active role in nurturing and bonding with their children. We discuss the benefits of involving fathers in all aspects of parenting, including caregiving, discipline, and emotional support, highlighting the positive impact it has on children's development.

We also explore the unique challenges faced by single fathers and provide support strategies to help them navigate the journey of parenting alone. The importance of flexibility and adaptability is discussed, recognizing that shared parenting requires constant adjustment and responsiveness to changing circumstances.

Guidance on handling conflicts and finding compromises as co-parents is provided, emphasising the need for open-mindedness and a focus on the best interests of the children. We explore the role of extended family members and support networks in sharing parenting responsibilities, recognizing the value of a strong support system.

The long-term benefits of shared parenting for children's development and overall well-being are discussed, highlighting the positive impact it has on their emotional, social, and cognitive growth. By embracing shared parenting, fathers and co-parents create an environment of stability, love, and support that nurtures children's full potential.

Sharing parenting responsibilities and partnering in parenthood can bring numerous benefits to both parents and children. However, it can also present challenges that require understanding, communication, and compromise. Let's explore some of the challenges faced by parents in sharing parenting and co-parenting, along with potential solutions and illustrations:

1. Unequal Distribution of Responsibilities:

Parents may struggle with an imbalance in parenting tasks, leading to feelings of resentment and exhaustion.

Solution: Open and honest communication is essential. Parents can have regular discussions to assess and adjust the distribution of responsibilities based on their individual strengths, availability, and preferences. Creating a shared parenting plan or schedule can help ensure a fair division of tasks.

Illustration: Krishnapriya and Mr Ram, a couple with different work schedules, sit down to discuss their parenting responsibilities. They realise that Mr Ram has been taking on a larger share of the household chores, while Krishnapriya primarily focuses on child care. By openly discussing their needs and preferences, they create a revised schedule that allows for a more balanced distribution of tasks.

2. Differences in Parenting Styles and Values:

Parents may have varying approaches to discipline, routines, and decision-making, leading to disagreements and conflicts.

Solution: Parents can engage in active listening and empathy to understand each other's perspectives. They can work together to establish common ground and develop a shared parenting philosophy that incorporates both partners' values. Regular communication and compromise are key to finding solutions that align with their parenting goals.

Illustration: Emily and James, a couple with different parenting styles, attend a parenting workshop together. Through open dialogue and guided discussions, they gain insights into each other's perspectives and learn effective strategies for merging their parenting styles. They gradually develop a cohesive approach that honours their individual values while creating a nurturing and consistent environment for their children.

3. Communication Breakdowns:

Busy schedules and external stressors can lead to miscommunication and misunderstandings between co-parents.

Solution: Regular and intentional communication is vital. Setting aside dedicated time to discuss parenting matters, actively listening to each other, and respecting each other's opinions can foster effective co-parenting. Utilising tools like shared calendars and parenting apps can help keep both partners informed and organised.

Illustration: Anupam and Jessica, a couple navigating co-parenting after separation, establish a weekly meeting to discuss their children's needs and coordinate schedules. They maintain open and respectful communication, sharing important updates and addressing any concerns promptly. By prioritising effective communication, they create a supportive co-parenting dynamic that promotes their children's well-being.

4. Balancing Work and Parenting: The demands of work can make it challenging for both parents to actively participate in parenting responsibilities.

Solution: Flexible work arrangements and shared decision-making can help parents manage their work commitments while remaining engaged in their children's lives. Both partners can support each other in achieving a healthy work-life balance by being understanding and providing assistance when needed.

Illustration: Mr Krishna and Krishnapriya, a dual-career couple, collaborate to find ways to balance work and parenting. They negotiate flexible work schedules, share child drop-off and pick-up duties, and take turns preparing meals. By prioritising open communication and a supportive approach, they successfully navigate the challenges of balancing work and parenting responsibilities.

5. Navigating Different Schedules and Commitments:

Each parent may have individual commitments and obligations outside of parenting, making it challenging to coordinate and synchronise schedules.

Solution: Regular planning and coordination are essential. Parents can create shared calendars, establish routines, and synchronise their schedules to ensure smooth transitions and effective co-parenting. Flexibility and compromise are key when accommodating each other's commitments.

Illustration: Mr Mohan and Lisa, a couple with demanding careers, collaborate to manage their busy schedules. They proactively plan and communicate to ensure they have designated time for family activities and prioritise their children's needs. By aligning their schedules and being flexible, they successfully navigate their individual commitments while maintaining a strong partnership in parenting.

By recognizing the challenges and implementing effective solutions, parents can create a supportive and cooperative parenting environment. Open communication, understanding, and willingness to adapt are crucial for successful co-parenting and shared parenting experiences.

Defying Expectations: Challenging Stereotypes in Fatherhood

In this section , we examine the societal expectations and stereotypes associated with fatherhood, acknowledging the limitations and negative consequences of adhering to traditional gender roles. We encourage readers to explore the concept of defying expectations and embracing their individuality in fatherhood.

Inspiring stories of fathers who have defied stereotypes and excelled in non-traditional parenting roles are shared, providing examples of how breaking free from societal norms can lead to personal growth and fulfilment as a father. We highlight the importance of self-expression and authenticity in fatherhood, emphasising that each father brings unique qualities and perspectives to their parenting journey.

We discuss the challenges and barriers faced by fathers who defy traditional norms, recognizing the potential judgement and resistance they may encounter. The role of support networks and communities in challenging stereotypes and providing encouragement is explored, underscoring the importance of finding like-minded individuals who can offer understanding and support.

Practical strategies for overcoming societal pressures and judgement in defying expectations are provided, empowering fathers to confidently navigate their own path in fatherhood. We discuss the positive influence of defying expectations on children's development, as they witness diverse and inclusive parenting models that challenge rigid gender roles.

We delve into the benefits of embracing diversity in fatherhood and creating inclusive parenting environments. The importance of open-mindedness and empathy is emphasised, as fathers play a crucial role in challenging stereotypes and fostering acceptance in their families and communities.

We highlight the role of education and awareness in promoting a more inclusive and understanding society. By actively challenging stereotypes and advocating for equality in fatherhood, fathers can contribute to a cultural shift that embraces diversity and eliminates harmful expectations.

Ultimately, we encourage fathers to embrace their unique qualities, interests, and parenting styles, regardless of societal expectations. By being authentic and true to themselves, fathers can become role models for their children, inspiring them to embrace their true selves and live without the constraints of stereotypes.

Defying expectations and challenging stereotypes in fatherhood can be both rewarding and challenging. Let's explore some of the challenges that fathers may face when defying traditional stereotypes, along with potential solutions and illustrations:

1. Societal Pressure and Judgment:

Fathers who challenge stereotypes may face criticism or judgement from others who hold traditional views on fatherhood.

Solution: Confidence and self-assurance are key. Fathers can develop a strong sense of self and embrace their unique parenting style. Surrounding themselves with a supportive network of like-minded individuals, such as friends, family, or parenting groups, can provide encouragement and validation.

Illustration: Mr Rahul, a stay-at-home father, often faces questions and judgement from acquaintances who question his decision to prioritise parenting over a career. However, Mr Rahul connects with other stay-at-home fathers through online communities and local support groups. By sharing experiences and offering support, they empower each other to confidently embrace their non-traditional roles.

2. Balancing Personal Identity:

Challenging stereotypes may require fathers to redefine their own identity and navigate the expectations they have for themselves.

Solution: Self-reflection and self-acceptance are crucial. Fathers can explore their values, passions, and aspirations beyond traditional gender roles. Engaging in activities that align with their interests and maintaining a sense of personal fulfilment can contribute to a balanced identity.

Illustration: Mr Krishna, a father who actively challenges stereotypes, feels conflicted between his role as a caregiver and his desire to pursue his career ambitions. Through self-reflection, he realises that both aspects are essential to his identity. By setting clear boundaries, communicating openly with his partner, and seeking support from others who have faced similar challenges, he finds a harmonious balance between fatherhood and personal growth.

3. Co-Parenting Dynamics:

Fathers who challenge stereotypes may encounter resistance or difficulties in establishing equitable co-parenting relationships.

Solution: Effective communication and shared decision-making are vital. Fathers can engage in open and respectful dialogue with their co-parent, focusing on the best interests of the children. Establishing clear roles, responsibilities, and expectations can contribute to a more balanced and harmonious co-parenting dynamic.

Illustration: Anupam and Rachel, a divorced couple, initially face challenges in establishing an equitable co-parenting arrangement. Anupam, as an involved and nurturing father, is committed to challenging stereotypes and maintaining an active role in his children's lives. Through ongoing communication, mediation, and a shared focus on their children's well-being, they develop a co-parenting plan that honours both parents' contributions and challenges traditional gender norms.

4. Navigating Work-Life Balance:

Challenging stereotypes may require fathers to navigate work-life balance in a society that often prioritises traditional gender roles.

Solution: Flexibility and boundary-setting are essential. Fathers can negotiate flexible work arrangements, communicate their needs to employers, and actively prioritise family time. Engaging in self-care activities and seeking support from their co-parent, family, or friends can also contribute to a healthier work-life balance.

Illustration: Mr Mohan, a father challenging stereotypes, faces pressure to conform to traditional expectations in his workplace. However, he advocates for a flexible work schedule that allows him to be present for his children's important moments. By effectively managing his time, setting boundaries, and demonstrating his commitment to both work and family, Mr Mohan gradually earns the respect and understanding of his colleagues and superiors.

By recognizing and addressing these challenges, fathers can successfully challenge stereotypes, embrace their unique roles, and create nurturing and supportive environments for their children. It requires resilience, self-confidence, open communication, and seeking support from like-minded individuals who share similar experiences.

Nurturing Individuality: Fostering Self-Expression in Fatherhood

In this section, we emphasise the importance of recognizing and celebrating the individuality of each child. We encourage fathers to support and nurture their children's unique interests and talents, creating a safe and supportive environment for self-expression.

We explore various forms of self-expression, such as creative arts, sports, hobbies, and personal style, recognizing that each child has their own distinct way of expressing themselves. Strategies are provided for fathers to encourage and empower their children to explore their passions, helping them discover their true selves.

Fostering individuality is discussed as a means to promote self-confidence and personal growth in children. We address challenges and societal pressures that may hinder a child's ability to express their individuality, highlighting the importance of fathers' active involvement in creating an inclusive and accepting space.

Open communication and active listening are emphasised as key components in understanding a child's desires and aspirations. By fostering open dialogue, fathers can better support their children's individuality and help them navigate any obstacles they may face.

We explore the impact of nurturing individuality on a child's overall well-being and happiness, recognizing that when children are allowed to be true to themselves, they experience greater fulfilment and a stronger sense of identity.

The role of fathers in promoting inclusivity and acceptance of diverse interests and identities is discussed, highlighting their responsibility in shaping a more tolerant society. We provide guidance on setting healthy boundaries while still encouraging self-expression, recognizing the importance of balance and respect.

We discuss the long-term impact of supporting a child's individuality on their future success and fulfilment, emphasising that when children are encouraged to be their authentic selves, they are more likely to pursue their passions and achieve their goals.

Personal stories and examples of fathers who have successfully nurtured their children's individuality are shared, providing inspiration and guidance. We explore the connection between self-expression and positive parent-child relationships, recognizing that supporting a child's individuality strengthens the bond between father and child.

Fathers are encouraged to embrace their own individuality as a positive example for their children. By modelling self-expression and authenticity, fathers can inspire their children to embrace their unique qualities and live life fully, unapologetically true to themselves.

Nurturing individuality and fostering self-expression in fatherhood is essential for allowing children to explore their unique identities. However, this can present challenges in various ways. Let's delve into some of the challenges fathers may encounter when trying to foster self-expression in their children, along with potential solutions and illustrations:

1. Social Expectations and Gender Norms:

Societal expectations and traditional gender norms can limit children's self-expression and encourage conformity.

Solution: Fathers can challenge gender stereotypes by promoting an open and inclusive environment where children feel free to express themselves authentically. They can provide diverse role models and expose their children to a wide range of interests and activities, regardless of societal expectations.

Illustration: Mr Ram, a father of a young boy named Ethan, actively challenges gender norms by encouraging Ethan to explore a variety of interests. Mr Ram exposes Ethan to both traditionally masculine and feminine activities, such as sports and arts, and supports his choices without judgement. By providing a nurturing and accepting environment, Mr Ram helps Ethan embrace his individuality and express himself freely.

2. Fear of Judgment and Bullying:

Parents may worry about their children facing judgement or bullying when expressing themselves in non-conforming ways.

Solution: Fathers can provide emotional support and guidance to help their children navigate potential challenges. By fostering open communication, fathers can encourage their children to share their feelings and experiences, allowing them to develop resilience and self-confidence.

Illustration: Daniel, a father of a teenage daughter named Lily, recognizes her passion for unconventional fashion and self-expression. Knowing that Lily may encounter criticism or bullying, Daniel has open conversations with her about the importance of staying true to herself. He encourages her to build a strong support network of friends and mentors who share her interests, fostering a sense of belonging and resilience against negativity.

3. Parental Expectations and Personal Biases:

Fathers may inadvertently impose their own expectations or biases on their children, limiting their self-expression.

Solution: Fathers can engage in self-reflection and self-awareness to identify and address their own biases. They can create a non-judgmental space where their children feel accepted and encouraged to explore their interests and passions.

Illustration: James, a father who initially had conservative views on his children's career choices, reflects on his biases and realises the importance of supporting their individuality. He actively listens to his children, engages in discussions about their aspirations, and encourages them to pursue their passions. By overcoming his own biases, James empowers his children to express themselves freely and pursue their unique paths.

4. Balancing Individuality and Values:

Fathers may struggle to balance nurturing their children's individuality while instilling core values and principles.

Solution: Fathers can engage in open dialogue with their children, discussing the importance of values and personal integrity. By providing guidance and setting boundaries within a framework of respect and understanding, fathers can support their children's self-expression while ensuring they navigate the world with a strong moral compass.

Illustration: Ryan, a father of twin boys, encourages their self-expression while emphasising the values of kindness and empathy. He discusses real-life scenarios and guides his children to understand the impact of their actions on others. Through this approach, Ryan nurtures their individuality while instilling values that promote positive social interactions.

By addressing these challenges and implementing solutions, fathers can create an environment that nurtures their children's individuality and fosters self-expression. It requires fathers to challenge societal norms, promote open communication, provide support, and continually reflect on their own beliefs and biases. Ultimately, by embracing their children's unique identities, fathers help them develop into confident, self-expressive individuals.

Cultivating Healthy Relationships: Building Strong Connections in Fatherhood

In this section, we delve into the significance of healthy relationships in a father's life and the lives of his children. We explore the role of fathers in fostering positive parent-child relationships, recognizing the profound impact these relationships have on a child's development and well-being.

We emphasise the importance of open communication, trust, and respect in building strong connections. Fathers are encouraged to create a nurturing and supportive environment for their children, where they feel safe to express themselves and share their thoughts and emotions.

Strategies are provided for fathers to actively engage with their children and dedicate quality time to strengthen the parent-child bond. We acknowledge the different stages of child development and discuss how fathers can adapt their parenting approach to cultivate healthy relationships at each stage, from infancy to adolescence.

We address the challenges and obstacles that may arise in building healthy relationships, offering guidance on overcoming them. We highlight the significance of empathy, understanding, and validation in fostering emotional connection with children, encouraging fathers to be present and attuned to their children's needs.

The role of fathers in promoting positive sibling relationships and healthy family dynamics is discussed, recognizing the interconnectedness of relationships within the family unit. We also explore the importance of building healthy relationships with extended family members and the broader community, recognizing the support and enriching experiences they can provide.

Guidance is provided on setting boundaries, establishing discipline, and maintaining a balance between authority and warmth in parent-child relationships. We emphasise the impact of positive role modelling and the importance of demonstrating healthy relationship dynamics for children to learn and emulate.

We explore the benefits of cultivating healthy relationships on a child's social and emotional development, recognizing that these relationships serve as a foundation for their overall well-being. Fathers are encouraged to teach and model conflict resolution skills, equipping their children with valuable tools for navigating relationships in their own lives.

Strategies are provided for fathers to navigate challenging conversations and address sensitive topics with their children, fostering open and honest communication. We address the significance of self-care and self-reflection in maintaining healthy relationships as a father, recognizing the importance of nurturing oneself in order to be present and available for others.

We discuss the lifelong impact of healthy parent-child relationships on a child's well-being and future relationships. Personal stories and examples of fathers who have successfully cultivated healthy relationships with their children are shared, offering inspiration and guidance.

Cultivating healthy relationships and building strong connections in fatherhood is crucial for the well-being and development of both fathers and their children. However, it can present challenges along the way. Let's explore some of the challenges fathers may face in building strong connections and nurturing healthy relationships with their children, along with potential solutions and illustrations:

1. Time Constraints and Work-Life Balance:

Busy work schedules and other commitments can limit the amount of time fathers have available to spend with their children.

Solution: Fathers can prioritise quality over quantity when it comes to spending time with their children. They can establish regular routines or designated time slots for bonding activities and ensure that the time spent together is focused, engaging, and meaningful.

Illustration: Mr Mohan, a father who works long hours, recognizes the importance of quality time with his children. Despite his demanding job, he carves out dedicated time each day to engage in activities that his children enjoy. Whether it's reading bedtime stories, playing sports, or cooking together, Mr Mohan ensures that the time they spend together is cherished and meaningful.

2. Communication Barriers:

Communication challenges, such as generation gaps, language barriers, or differences in communication styles, can hinder effective interaction between fathers and their children.

Solution: Fathers can actively work on improving their communication skills and finding common ground with their children. They can listen attentively, show empathy, and adapt their communication style to meet the unique needs of each child.

Illustration: Miguel, a father who migrated to a new country with a different language, faces communication challenges with his children. To overcome this barrier, Miguel takes language classes and engages in activities that transcend language, such as playing music together or engaging in physical activities. By finding alternative ways to connect, Miguel strengthens his relationship with his children despite the communication obstacles.

3. Past Trauma or Family History:

Fathers may carry unresolved trauma or negative family experiences that can impact their ability to cultivate healthy relationships with their children.

Solution: Fathers can seek professional support, such as therapy or counselling, to address their own unresolved issues and heal past wounds. By actively working on their own well-being, fathers can break the cycle of generational trauma and create a nurturing environment for their children.

Illustration: Jason, a father who experienced a difficult childhood, recognizes the impact it has on his ability to build healthy relationships with his children. He seeks therapy to address his own trauma and learns healthy coping mechanisms to manage his emotions. Through this process, Jason creates a safe and supportive environment for his children, breaking the cycle of negative family history.

4. Parenting Styles and Conflict Resolution:

Differences in parenting styles and disagreements on discipline or other aspects of parenting can create tensions within father-child relationships.

Solution: Fathers can engage in open and respectful communication with their co-parent or spouse to establish consistent and mutually agreed-upon parenting approaches. They can also involve their children in discussions about expectations, boundaries, and problem-solving to foster a sense of ownership and collaboration.

Illustration: Adam, a father who co-parents with his ex-partner, faces challenges in aligning their parenting styles. Adam and his ex-partner regularly communicate and find compromises to ensure a consistent approach for their children. They involve their children in discussions, giving them a voice and helping them understand the reasoning behind decisions. Through collaborative problem-solving, Adam fosters healthy relationships with his children while maintaining a respectful co-parenting dynamic.

By acknowledging and addressing these challenges, fathers can overcome obstacles and cultivate healthy relationships with their children. It requires intention, commitment, and adaptability to navigate the complexities of fatherhood. Through meaningful engagement, effective communication, and a willingness to address personal and relational challenges, fathers can build strong connections and foster healthy relationships that endure.

Seeking Support: Navigating Challenges and Finding Help in Fatherhood

In this section, we acknowledge the importance of seeking support as a father and the benefits it brings to both fathers and their families. We explore the various challenges and pressures that fathers may face in different aspects of their lives, including work, relationships, and parenting, recognizing the impact these challenges can have on their well-being and ability to thrive as fathers.

We discuss the significance of addressing stress, burnout, and mental health concerns in fatherhood, emphasising the need for fathers to prioritise self-care. Understanding that seeking support is an essential part of self-care, we provide insights on the different types of support available, including emotional, practical, and informational support.

The role of support networks is explored, highlighting the importance of friends, family, and other fathers in providing guidance, encouragement, and a sense of belonging. We emphasise the value of open communication and vulnerability in seeking support and building meaningful connections with others who can relate to and understand the challenges of fatherhood.

Guidance is provided on identifying and accessing relevant resources and services for fathers, such as parenting classes, counselling, and community programs. We address common myths and misconceptions about seeking support and promote a culture of openness and acceptance in fatherhood, encouraging fathers to overcome any stigma or barriers that may hinder them from reaching out for help.

Personal stories and experiences of fathers who have sought support are shared, illustrating the positive impact it has had on their well-being and parenting journey. These stories serve as inspiration and provide validation for fathers who may be hesitant to seek support.

We discuss strategies for overcoming barriers to seeking support, including addressing stigma, time constraints, and cultural norms. We explore the benefits of peer support groups and online communities, which allow fathers to share experiences, seek advice, and find camaraderie in a non-judgmental space.

The role of professional support is also discussed, emphasising the value of therapists, coaches, and mentors in providing specialised guidance and helping fathers navigate specific challenges they may face.

Tips are provided for effective communication with partners, family members, and friends when seeking support and expressing needs. We acknowledge the importance of self-reflection and self-awareness in recognizing when support is needed and taking proactive steps to seek it.

We highlight the positive impact of seeking support on overall well-being, parenting skills, and the quality of father-child relationships. By seeking support, fathers can enhance their ability to navigate challenges, build resilience, and create a nurturing environment for their children.

Seeking support as a father is essential for navigating challenges and finding help in fatherhood. However, it can present various challenges that fathers may encounter. Let's explore some of these challenges along with potential solutions and illustrations:

1. Stigma and Societal Expectations:

There may be societal expectations that fathers should be self-reliant and have all the answers, making it difficult for them to reach out for support without feeling judged or stigmatised.

Solution: Fathers can challenge societal norms by normalising the act of seeking support and openly discussing their challenges. By sharing their experiences and encouraging conversations around fatherhood, fathers can create a supportive environment where seeking help is seen as a sign of strength rather than weakness.

Illustration: Mr Ram, a father who initially felt hesitant to seek support due to societal expectations, decided to share his parenting journey on social media. By openly discussing his challenges, seeking advice, and sharing resources, Mr Ram not only found support from other fathers but also inspired a community of fathers to break the stigma and seek help when needed.

2. Lack of Awareness and Resources:

Fathers may face challenges in finding relevant support resources and services that cater specifically to their needs.

Solution: Fathers can proactively seek out resources and support networks that are tailored to their experiences. They can research online platforms, community organisations, and local support groups that provide guidance, information, and a sense of camaraderie for fathers.

Illustration: Mr Krishna, a new father, found it challenging to locate resources specific to fatherhood in his area. He decided to reach out to his local community centre and proposed the idea of a fatherhood support group. With the support of the community centre, Mr Krishna created a space where fathers could come together, share experiences, and access valuable resources that were previously lacking in their community.

3. Time Constraints and Balancing Priorities:

Fathers often juggle multiple responsibilities, including work, household tasks, and parenting, which can make it challenging to find the time and energy to seek support.

Solution: Fathers can prioritise self-care and carve out dedicated time for seeking support. They can communicate their needs and concerns with their partners or family members, allowing for the necessary support and understanding to create space for self-care and personal growth.

Illustration: James, a father with a demanding job, struggled to find time for self-care and seeking support. He recognized the importance of self-care in being a present and engaged father. James and his partner established a shared schedule that allowed both of them to have dedicated time for self-care and personal pursuits, ensuring they had the energy and capacity to seek support when needed.

4. Limited Support Networks:

Fathers may find it challenging to establish or access support networks, especially if they feel isolated or have limited connections with other fathers.

Solution: Fathers can actively seek out opportunities to connect with other fathers through parenting classes, community events, online forums, or social media groups. They can also initiate conversations with other fathers they meet in various settings, creating opportunities for shared experiences and support.

Illustration: Robert, a stay-at-home father, struggled with feelings of isolation as he had limited interactions with other fathers in his neighbourhood. He decided to organise a regular playgroup for fathers and their children in the community park. This initiative not only provided a supportive network for fathers but also allowed children to bond and grow together.

By acknowledging and addressing these challenges, fathers can navigate the complexities of seeking support and finding help in fatherhood. It requires breaking down societal barriers, actively seeking resources, prioritising self-care, and creating support networks. Through these efforts, fathers can find the support they need to navigate challenges, grow as individuals, and foster positive relationships with their children.

Raising Empathetic Children: Fostering Compassion and Understanding

In this section, we delve into the importance of empathy in children's development and the positive impact it has on their relationships and social interactions. We explore the benefits of raising empathetic children, including increased emotional intelligence, better conflict resolution skills, and a sense of social responsibility.

We discuss the crucial role parents play in modelling empathy and cultivating an empathetic household environment. By demonstrating empathy in our own actions and interactions, we provide a powerful example for our children to follow. We also provide strategies for teaching empathy to children, such as encouraging perspective-taking, active listening, and recognizing emotions in others.

Open communication and dialogue are emphasised as key elements in fostering empathy. We discuss the importance of discussing emotions, diversity, and social issues with children, as these conversations help them develop a deeper understanding and empathy for others. We also explore the connection between empathy and kindness, providing practical ways to encourage acts of kindness in children's daily lives.

Recognizing the significance of self-empathy, we discuss the importance of teaching children to be empathetic towards themselves. This includes fostering self-compassion and self-awareness, allowing children to develop a healthy relationship with their own emotions and needs.

The impact of media and technology on empathy development is explored, and we provide guidelines for promoting empathy in digital environments. We address common challenges in raising empathetic children, such as handling conflicts, dealing with bullying, and navigating friendships, offering guidance on how to approach these situations with empathy and understanding.

We discuss the role of schools and communities in fostering empathy and explore ways to collaborate with educators and community organisations to create environments that promote empathy. We also discuss the importance of addressing biases and stereotypes with children, promoting inclusivity, and celebrating diversity.

Recognizing the power of literature, storytelling, and media, we explore how these tools can be used to promote empathy and help children understand different perspectives. We discuss the role of empathy in resolving conflicts and promoting peaceful relationships, both within the family and in the wider community.

Personal stories and experiences of parents who have successfully nurtured empathy in their children are shared, highlighting the positive impact it has had on their lives. We emphasise that fostering empathy is an ongoing process, requiring consistent reinforcement and the recognition of empathetic behaviours.

Guidance is provided on addressing challenges and setbacks in the development of empathy in children, promoting resilience and perseverance. We explore the connection between empathy and social justice, and discuss ways to empower children to make a positive difference in the world through empathy and action.

Raising empathetic children and fostering compassion and understanding can present challenges for parents. Let's explore some of these challenges along with potential solutions and illustrations:

1. Limited Role Models:

In a society that sometimes emphasises individualism or lacks diverse and empathetic role models, parents may find it challenging to provide their children with positive examples of empathy.

Solution: Parents can actively seek out diverse role models, both within their immediate community and through media, who demonstrate empathy and compassion. They can expose their children to stories, books, movies, and real-life experiences that highlight acts of empathy and encourage discussions around empathy and understanding.

Illustration: Krishnapriya, a mother, noticed a lack of empathetic role models in her neighbourhood. She decided to organise a community event where individuals from different backgrounds and professions shared their stories of empathy and kindness. This event not only exposed children to various perspectives but also inspired them to develop their own empathetic behaviours.

2. Balancing Discipline and Empathy:

Parents may struggle to find a balance between setting boundaries and disciplining their children while also nurturing empathy and understanding.

Solution: Parents can adopt a balanced approach by setting clear expectations and consequences while also emphasising empathy and understanding. They can explain the reasons behind rules and discipline, encourage open communication, and provide opportunities for their children to practise empathy in their daily lives.

Illustration: Mr Mohan, a father, faced a challenge in balancing discipline and empathy with his teenage son. Instead of solely focusing on punishment for negative behaviour, Mr Mohan initiated conversations with his son to understand the underlying emotions and address them empathetically. By incorporating empathy into discipline, Mr Mohan strengthened his son's understanding of consequences and developed his empathy skills.

3. Addressing Peer Influence:

Children may face pressure from peers or societal norms that discourage empathy and compassion, making it challenging for parents to instil these values.

Solution: Parents can foster open communication with their children, actively listen to their concerns, and discuss the importance of empathy in navigating peer interactions. They can encourage their children to choose friends who share their values and provide guidance on standing up for others and showing empathy in challenging situations.

Illustration: Emma, a parent, discovered that her child was facing peer pressure to exclude a classmate. Emma engaged in open dialogue with her child, explaining the impact of exclusion and encouraging empathy towards others. Together, they brainstormed ways to support their classmates and foster a more inclusive environment.

4. Navigating Media Influence:

Children are exposed to various forms of media that may not always promote empathy and understanding. Parents may struggle with helping their children navigate media messages and develop critical thinking skills.

Solution: Parents can actively engage with their children's media consumption, discussing the messages portrayed and encouraging them to think critically about empathy, stereotypes, and biases. They can guide their children towards media that promotes empathy and provides positive examples of compassionate behaviour.

Illustration: Anupam, a parent, noticed the negative impact of certain media on his child's empathy. He implemented media guidelines in their household, discussing the importance of consuming content that portrays empathy and demonstrating alternatives that promote understanding and inclusivity.

By addressing these challenges and implementing solutions, parents can navigate the journey of raising empathetic children. It requires intentional efforts, modelling empathy, providing diverse role models, balancing discipline with empathy, addressing peer influence, and guiding children through media consumption. Through these approaches, parents can nurture their children's empathy, fostering a more compassionate and understanding future generation.

A Note On How to Talk Empathy And Its Importance

When I mention "discussing empathy," it refers to engaging in conversations with children about the concept of empathy, its importance, and how it can be demonstrated in their interactions with others. Here are some aspects of empathy that can be discussed:

1. **Definition of Empathy:** Start by explaining what empathy means. Empathy is the ability to understand and share the feelings of others. It involves recognizing and acknowledging the emotions someone else is experiencing and showing care and concern towards them.

2. **Recognizing Emotions**: Help children understand different emotions and how they may manifest in others. Discuss various facial expressions, body language, and verbal cues that indicate how someone might be feeling. Encourage children to pay attention to these cues and develop sensitivity to others' emotional states.

3. **Perspective-Taking**: Discuss the importance of putting oneself in someone else's shoes to understand their experiences and feelings. Help children understand that everyone has unique perspectives shaped by their background, experiences, and emotions. Encourage them to consider how they would feel in a similar situation and how their actions might impact others.

4. **Active Listening**: Teach children the importance of attentive and active listening when someone is sharing their feelings or experiences. Encourage them to listen without interrupting and to respond with empathy, validating the other person's emotions.

5. **Responding with Empathy:** Discuss different ways children can respond empathetically to others. This can include offering comforting

words, showing understanding, offering help or support, or simply being present and attentive.

6. **Kindness and Compassion**: Connect empathy to acts of kindness and compassion. Explain that empathy can lead to actions that make a positive difference in someone's life. Encourage children to engage in acts of kindness, such as helping a friend in need or standing up against bullying.

7. **Embracing Diversity and Inclusion**: Discuss the importance of empathy in understanding and appreciating people from diverse backgrounds, cultures, and experiences. Help children recognize the value of inclusivity and empathy in fostering positive relationships and creating a harmonious community.

It's crucial to have ongoing conversations about empathy with children, as it helps them develop a deeper understanding and appreciation for the emotions and experiences of others. By discussing empathy, parents can encourage their children to cultivate empathy as a core value and integrate it into their interactions with family, friends, and the broader world.

Embracing Fatherhood: The Journey of Becoming a Father

Becoming a father is a transformative experience that profoundly impacts a man's life. In this chapter, we explore the emotional and psychological aspects of embracing fatherhood, including the joys, fears, and challenges that come with it.

We discuss the importance of active involvement in parenting and the role of fathers in nurturing their children's growth and development. Fatherhood goes beyond providing for the physical needs of a child—it involves building a deep emotional connection and being actively present in their lives.

We examine both traditional and evolving societal expectations of fathers, recognizing the changing dynamics of fatherhood in modern times. Fathers are increasingly taking on roles that go beyond the traditional breadwinner, becoming more involved in caregiving and household responsibilities. We celebrate the diversity of fatherhood experiences and the unique contributions each father brings to his family.

Building a strong bond with one's children is essential, and we discuss the importance of quality time, active listening, and open communication. By being attentive and engaged, fathers create a safe and nurturing environment that supports their children's emotional well-being and development.

Self-reflection and personal growth play a significant role in becoming a better father. We encourage fathers to examine their own upbringing, values, and beliefs, and to strive for continuous learning and self-improvement. Through introspection, fathers can better understand themselves and their impact on their children's lives.

We address common parenting challenges and provide practical strategies for navigating them. Discipline, setting boundaries, and balancing work and family life are common areas of concern for fathers. By sharing effective approaches and emphasising the importance of flexibility and adaptability, we empower fathers to overcome these challenges.

A supportive and equal partnership with the co-parent or spouse is crucial in sharing parenting responsibilities. We discuss the importance of open communication, mutual respect, and teamwork in creating a harmonious parenting dynamic.

Fatherhood has a significant impact on personal identity, relationships, and self-care. We explore the challenges fathers face in maintaining a healthy work-life balance and emphasise the importance of self-care and well-being. By prioritising their own physical and mental health, fathers can better meet the needs of their families.

Being a positive role model is paramount in fatherhood. We discuss the values of empathy, integrity, and respect, and encourage fathers to embody these qualities. Children learn by observing their fathers' actions, and fathers have the power to shape their children's character and values.

We recognize that fatherhood experiences vary depending on family structure. We explore the unique challenges faced by single fathers, same-sex parents, and blended families, offering support and guidance tailored to their specific circumstances.

The role of extended family and community in supporting fathers is vital. We discuss the importance of building a network of support and accessing available resources. By fostering connections with other fathers and seeking guidance from experienced individuals, fathers can navigate the challenges of fatherhood more effectively.

Creating lasting memories and traditions with one's children is significant. We explore the impact these shared experiences have on a child's sense of belonging and identity, strengthening the bond between father and child.

We address the emotional aspects of fatherhood, including the experience of unconditional love, the fear of failure, and the importance of vulnerability. Fathers are encouraged to embrace their emotions and seek support when needed, recognizing that vulnerability is a strength.

Fatherhood is a journey of ongoing learning and adaptation. We discuss the importance of being open to new perspectives and embracing the ever-changing needs of children. By staying curious and engaged, fathers can continue to grow alongside their children.

The impact of fatherhood on the father-child relationship is explored throughout different stages of a child's life, from infancy to adulthood. We discuss the importance of evolving relationships and adjusting parenting approaches to meet the changing needs of children.

Finally, we reflect on the legacy of fatherhood and the lasting impact fathers have on their children's lives. By shaping their values, beliefs, and future aspirations, fathers leave a profound imprint on their children's paths, contributing to the next generation's growth and development.

Certainly! Becoming a father and embracing fatherhood is a transformative journey that can come with various challenges. Here are some common challenges that fathers may face along with potential solutions and illustrations:

1. Balancing Responsibilities:

Fathers often struggle to balance their responsibilities as parents with other aspects of their lives, such as work and personal commitments. This can lead to feelings of overwhelm and stress.

Solution: Time management and prioritisation are key. Fathers can create a schedule that allows them to allocate dedicated time for both their children and their other responsibilities. This may involve setting boundaries at work, involving their co-parent or extended family in childcare duties, and seeking support from others when needed.

Illustration: Mr Rahul, a new father, found it challenging to balance his demanding job and spending time with his child. He decided to have an open conversation with his employer about his desire for work-life balance and negotiated a flexible schedule that allowed him to be more present for his child.

2. Adjusting to Parenting Roles:

Fathers may find it challenging to navigate their role as a parent, particularly if they have limited experience or societal expectations differ from their own values. They may question their abilities and feel uncertain about how to best support their children.

Solution: Active learning and seeking guidance can be helpful. Fathers can attend parenting classes or workshops, read books on parenting, or join support groups to gain knowledge and exchange experiences with other fathers. They can also engage in open communication with their co-parent to align on parenting approaches and seek their partner's guidance and insights.

Illustration: Mr Mohan, a first-time father, felt overwhelmed by the responsibility of caring for his newborn. He actively sought out parenting resources, attended parenting workshops, and joined a support group for new fathers. These efforts helped him gain confidence in his role and provided valuable insights from other fathers who had faced similar challenges.

3. Dealing with Societal Expectations:

Fathers may face societal pressures and stereotypes that dictate what a "good" father should be like. These expectations can create stress and self-doubt, as they may feel the need to conform to rigid definitions of masculinity and fatherhood.

Solution: Challenging societal norms and embracing individuality is important. Fathers can redefine what it means to be a good father based on their own values, beliefs, and the unique needs of their children. By focusing on their genuine connection with their children and nurturing their individuality, fathers can find fulfilment and break free from societal constraints.

Illustration: Mr Krishna, a stay-at-home father, faced criticism and judgement from others who believed that fathers should be the primary breadwinners. Despite the societal pressure, he remained committed to his role as an involved and nurturing father. He embraced his own definition of fatherhood and focused on creating a loving and supportive environment for his children.

4. Self-Care and Well-being:

Fathers often neglect their own self-care and well-being while prioritising the needs of their children and family. This can lead to exhaustion, burnout, and a decline in overall well-being.

Solution: Prioritising self-care is crucial. Fathers should engage in activities that promote their physical and mental well-being, such as exercise, hobbies, spending time with friends, and seeking support when needed. They should also communicate their needs with their co-parent and establish a support system to share parenting responsibilities.

Illustration: Anupam, a father of two, realised the importance of self-care after experiencing burnout. He started setting aside time for himself each week, whether it was going for a run, practising mindfulness, or pursuing his hobbies. By prioritising self-care, he became a happier and more present father for his children.

Remember, every father's journey is unique, and the challenges they face may vary. By recognizing these challenges and implementing appropriate solutions, fathers can navigate the complexities of embracing fatherhood and create fulfilling relationships with their children.

CHAPTER FIVE

Frequently Asked Questions

1. What are the essential qualities of a good father?

A good father possesses qualities such as love, patience, understanding, and commitment. However, a mistake some fathers make is being too strict or distant, which can result in strained relationships with their children and a lack of emotional connection. The aftereffect of this mistake may include children feeling misunderstood, distant, or even resentful towards their fathers.

2. How can fathers balance their work and family responsibilities?

Balancing work and family responsibilities requires effective time management and prioritisation. One mistake fathers sometimes make is prioritising work over family, neglecting quality time and important family events. This can lead to feelings of neglect and a strained relationship with their children and partner. The aftereffect may include a lack of connection, resentment, and a sense of feeling unimportant or undervalued.

3. What are some effective strategies for disciplining children?

Effective discipline involves setting clear expectations, consistent enforcement of rules, and using positive reinforcement. However, a mistake fathers can make is being too harsh or punitive in their discipline approach, which can lead to fear, resentment, and a strained parent-child relationship. The aftereffect may include children feeling insecure, anxious, or rebellious.

4. How can fathers build a strong emotional bond with their children?

Building a strong emotional bond requires active listening, quality time, and open communication. A mistake fathers may make is not prioritising emotional connection, focusing solely on providing material needs instead. This can result in a lack of emotional intimacy and understanding between father and child. The aftereffect may include children feeling emotionally distant, seeking validation elsewhere, or struggling with trust issues.

5. What role does a father play in their child's education?

Fathers play a vital role in their child's education by providing support, encouragement, and involvement. However, a mistake fathers can make is being disengaged or not valuing education as much as other aspects of their child's life. This can lead to a lack of motivation, academic struggles, and a sense of disconnection between father and child. The aftereffect may include children feeling unsupported, undervalued, or uninterested in their educational pursuits.

6. How can fathers support their partner during pregnancy and childbirth?

Fathers can support their partners during pregnancy and childbirth by being actively involved, providing emotional support, and participating in prenatal classes and doctor's appointments. However, a mistake some fathers make is not fully understanding or empathising with the physical and emotional challenges their partners may face. This can lead to feelings of isolation, frustration, and a lack of support for the mother. The aftereffect may include strained communication, feelings of resentment, and a potential impact on the overall well-being of both parents.

7. What are some ways to effectively communicate with children of different ages?

Effective communication with children of different ages involves adjusting communication styles, actively listening, and providing age-appropriate information. However, a mistake fathers may make is not adapting their communication style to suit the developmental stage of their child. This can result in miscommunication, misunderstandings, and difficulty in connecting with their children. The aftereffect may include strained relationships, a lack of trust, and potential behavioural or emotional challenges.

8. How can fathers handle the challenges of parenting a teenager?

Handling the challenges of parenting a teenager requires open communication, setting boundaries, and maintaining a supportive environment. However, a mistake fathers may make is being overly controlling or dismissive of their teenager's autonomy and individuality. This can lead to rebellion, resentment, and strained parent-child relationships. The aftereffect may include communication breakdowns, emotional distance, and potential long-term consequences on the teenager's self-esteem and decision-making abilities.

9. What are the benefits of involving fathers in childcare and household tasks?

Involving fathers in childcare and household tasks promotes shared responsibility, strengthens family bonds, and provides positive role modelling. However, a mistake some fathers make is assuming a passive role or not actively engaging in childcare and household duties. This can result in an unequal distribution of labour, increased stress on the mother, and a missed opportunity for fathers to develop a strong bond with their children. The aftereffect may include feelings of resentment, relationship strain, and a lack of appreciation for the father's involvement.

10. How can fathers prioritise self-care while taking care of their family?

Prioritising self-care as a father is crucial for maintaining physical and mental well-being. It involves setting boundaries, seeking support, and engaging in activities that promote relaxation and personal growth. However, a mistake fathers may make is neglecting their own needs and sacrificing their well-being for the sake of their family. This can lead to burnout, increased stress levels, and potential negative impacts on their overall health. The aftereffect may include reduced emotional availability, decreased patience, and potential strain on relationships within the family unit.

11. How can fathers support their child's mental and emotional well-being?

Fathers can support their child's mental and emotional well-being by providing a safe and nurturing environment, actively listening, and validating their feelings. However, a mistake fathers may make is dismissing or invalidating their child's emotions, which can lead to emotional suppression, insecurity, and a strained relationship. The aftereffect may include difficulty in expressing emotions, challenges in forming trusting relationships, and potential long-term impacts on mental health.

12. What are some tips for co-parenting after divorce or separation?

Co-parenting after divorce or separation requires effective communication, mutual respect, and prioritising the child's well-being. However, a mistake fathers may make is engaging in conflicts or using their child as a messenger between parents. This can lead to increased stress, confusion, and emotional turmoil for the child. The aftereffect may include feelings of guilt, loyalty conflicts, and potential negative impacts on the child's emotional and psychological development.

13. How can fathers promote gender equality and healthy attitudes towards relationships?

Fathers can promote gender equality and healthy attitudes towards relationships by modelling respectful behaviour, challenging stereotypes, and encouraging open dialogue. However, a mistake fathers may make is perpetuating gender biases or engaging in sexist attitudes, which can impact their children's perceptions and beliefs. The aftereffect may include the reinforcement of gender stereotypes, unequal power dynamics, and potential negative impacts on the child's self-esteem and relationships.

14. What are the best ways to handle conflicts and disagreements with a child?

Handling conflicts and disagreements with a child requires active listening, empathy, and finding constructive solutions. However, a mistake fathers may make is resorting to authoritarian or aggressive approaches, which can escalate conflicts, damage trust, and hinder effective communication. The aftereffect may include strained parent-child relationships, resentment, and potential long-term impacts on the child's ability to resolve conflicts in a healthy manner.

15. How can fathers positively influence their child's values and morals?

Fathers can positively influence their child's values and morals by embodying and promoting positive character traits, engaging in ethical discussions, and providing guidance. However, a mistake fathers may make is imposing their own values without considering their child's individuality or fostering open-mindedness. This can lead to resistance, rebellion, and a lack of autonomy in moral decision-making. The aftereffect may include strained relationships, a sense of identity suppression, and potential long-term impacts on the child's moral development.

16. How can fathers navigate the challenges of raising a child with special needs?

Navigating the challenges of raising a child with special needs requires patience, understanding, and seeking support. However, a mistake fathers may make is feeling overwhelmed or isolated, which can lead to decreased involvement and emotional detachment. The aftereffect may include a strained relationship with the child, feelings of guilt, and a lack of support for the child's unique needs.

17. How can fathers encourage their children's independence while ensuring their safety?

Fathers can encourage their children's independence by providing age-appropriate opportunities for growth, fostering decision-making skills, and setting clear boundaries. However, a mistake fathers may make is being overly protective or controlling, which can hinder the child's development of independence and self-confidence. The aftereffect may include a fear of taking risks, low self-esteem, and strained relationships due to a lack of trust.

18. What are some effective ways to bond with teenage children?

Bonding with teenage children requires active listening, respect for their autonomy, and engaging in activities they enjoy. However, a mistake fathers may make is not adapting their approach to meet the changing needs of their teenagers, resulting in a communication gap and disconnection. The aftereffect may include a strained relationship, decreased trust, and missed opportunities for mutual understanding and support.

19. How can fathers promote healthy body image and self-esteem in their children?

Fathers can promote healthy body image and self-esteem by emphasising the importance of inner qualities, encouraging a balanced approach to physical health, and refraining from making negative comments about appearance. However, a mistake fathers may make is unintentionally reinforcing societal beauty standards or engaging in body-shaming behaviour, which can negatively impact their child's self-perception and self-worth. The aftereffect may include body dissatisfaction, low self-esteem, and potential development of disordered eating or other unhealthy behaviours.

20. How can fathers help their children navigate peer pressure and make wise choices?

Fathers can help their children navigate peer pressure by fostering open communication, teaching critical thinking skills, and providing guidance on making informed decisions. However, a mistake fathers may make is being too controlling or dismissive of their child's social interactions, leading to a lack of trust and communication breakdown. The aftereffect may include isolation, risky behaviour, and strained relationships with both peers and fathers.

21. How can fathers support their children's career aspirations and goals?

Fathers can support their children's career aspirations and goals by providing encouragement, offering guidance, and helping them explore different opportunities. However, a mistake fathers may make is imposing their own career expectations or discouraging non-traditional career paths, which can lead to dissatisfaction, lack of fulfilment, and strained relationships. The aftereffect may include a diminished sense of autonomy, limited career prospects, and potential resentment towards their fathers.

22. How can fathers navigate the challenges of co-parenting in blended families?

Navigating the challenges of co-parenting in blended families requires effective communication, flexibility, and respect for all family members. However, a mistake fathers may make is prioritising their own biological children over their stepchildren, which can lead to feelings of favouritism, exclusion, and a fragmented family dynamic. The aftereffect may include resentment, strained relationships, and potential negative impacts on the well-being of all family members.

23. How can fathers address and prevent bullying in their children's lives?

Fathers can address and prevent bullying by promoting empathy, teaching conflict resolution skills, and fostering a supportive and inclusive environment. However, a mistake fathers may make is ignoring or minimising instances of bullying, which can lead to feelings of powerlessness, diminished self-esteem, and ongoing victimisation. The aftereffect may include emotional trauma, social isolation, and potential long-term effects on the child's mental health.

24. How can fathers support their children's emotional intelligence and social skills?

Fathers can support their children's emotional intelligence and social skills by modelling and encouraging empathy, teaching emotional regulation, and providing opportunities for social interactions. However, a mistake fathers may make is dismissing or invalidating their child's emotions, which can hinder emotional development, create communication barriers, and lead to difficulties in forming healthy relationships. The aftereffect may include emotional withdrawal, low self-esteem, and challenges in navigating social situations.

25. How can fathers foster a sense of cultural identity and heritage in their children?

Fathers can foster a sense of cultural identity and heritage in their children by sharing family traditions, teaching about their cultural background, and celebrating cultural events. However, a mistake fathers may make is neglecting or disregarding their child's multicultural identity, which can lead to a loss of connection to their roots, identity confusion, and a sense of not belonging. The aftereffect may include cultural disconnection, internal conflict, and potential difficulty in embracing diversity.

26. How can fathers teach their children about financial responsibility?

Fathers can teach their children about financial responsibility by providing age-appropriate lessons on budgeting, saving, and making wise financial decisions. However, a mistake fathers may make is shielding their children from financial realities or indulging their every desire, which can lead to entitlement, poor money management skills, and potential financial struggles in adulthood. The aftereffect may include financial dependency, limited financial literacy, and challenges in achieving financial stability.

27. How can fathers help their children develop resilience and cope with setbacks?

Fathers can help their children develop resilience by teaching problem-solving skills, encouraging a growth mindset, and providing emotional support during challenging times. However, a mistake fathers may make is overprotecting their children from failure or shielding them from adversity, which can hinder their resilience-building process. The aftereffect may include a fear of failure, low self-confidence, and difficulty in handling setbacks effectively.

28. How can fathers support their children's educational journey?

Fathers can support their children's educational journey by demonstrating the importance of education, providing resources for learning, and actively engaging in their academic pursuits. However, a mistake fathers may make is placing excessive pressure on their children to achieve academic success or micromanaging their educational experience, which can lead to anxiety, burnout, and a strained parent-child relationship. The aftereffect may include decreased motivation, performance anxiety, and potential long-term impacts on their educational and career development.

29. How can fathers promote healthy relationships with technology and screen time?

Fathers can promote healthy relationships with technology and screen time by setting limits, modelling responsible digital behaviour, and encouraging offline activities. However, a mistake fathers may make is allowing excessive screen time or using technology as a means of distraction or substitute for parenting, which can lead to addiction, social isolation, and impaired development of real-world relationships. The aftereffect may include decreased social skills, difficulty in self-regulation, and potential negative impacts on mental and physical health.

30. How can fathers foster a sense of adventure and curiosity in their children?

Fathers can foster a sense of adventure and curiosity in their children by encouraging exploration, supporting their interests, and providing opportunities for new experiences. However, a mistake fathers may make is being overly cautious or discouraging risk-taking, which can stifle creativity, limit personal growth, and hinder the development of a curious mindset. The aftereffect may include a fear of trying new things, limited self-expression, and potential missed opportunities for learning and personal development.

By being mindful of these potential mistakes and their aftereffects, fathers can navigate the challenges of parenthood with empathy, understanding, and a commitment to nurturing their children's growth, well-being, and future success.

CHAPTER SIX

WHAT MAKES YOUR CHILD HAPPY:MYTHS AND FACTS: UNVEILING MISCONCEPTIONS

Myth: Material possessions and lavish gifts bring happiness.

Fact: While material possessions may provide temporary joy, true happiness comes from meaningful experiences, emotional connection, and a supportive environment. Spending quality time with your child, engaging in activities together, and creating lasting memories are more effective ways to foster happiness.

Myth: Shielding your child from negative experiences and emotions will make them happier.

Fact: Shielding your child from negative experiences and emotions can hinder their emotional development. It is important to teach children how to cope with challenges, handle setbacks, and express their emotions in healthy ways. By providing guidance and support during difficult times, you can help them develop resilience and emotional intelligence.

Myth: Always saying "yes" and giving in to your child's demands will make them happy.

Fact: Constantly giving in to your child's every demand can create unrealistic expectations and a sense of entitlement. Setting appropriate boundaries, teaching delayed gratification, and helping your child understand the value of effort and hard work can foster a sense of accomplishment and genuine happiness.

Myth: Comparing your child to others and pressuring them to excel will make them happier.

Fact: Constantly comparing your child to others and pressuring them to excel can lead to anxiety, low self-esteem, and a fear of failure. Each child is unique, with their own strengths and abilities. Supporting their individual interests, encouraging personal growth, and celebrating their achievements, no matter how small, can contribute to their overall happiness.

Myth: Sacrificing your own happiness for your child's sake will make them happier.

Fact: Neglecting your own happiness and well-being can lead to burnout and negatively impact your ability to be present and supportive for your child. Taking care of yourself, pursuing your own interests, and maintaining a healthy work-life balance are essential for your own happiness, which in turn positively influences your child's well-being.

Myth: Providing constant entertainment and stimulation will make your child happier.

Fact: While it's important to engage your child in stimulating activities, it's equally important to allow them to experience boredom and develop their own creativity and problem-solving skills. Giving your child the space and freedom to explore their own interests and imagination can contribute to their overall happiness and sense of self-fulfilment.

Myth: Being a perfect parent is necessary for your child's happiness.

Fact: No one is a perfect parent, and striving for perfection can create unnecessary pressure and stress. It's more important to focus on creating a loving and supportive environment, fostering open communication, and being there for your child through both their successes and challenges. Your presence, understanding, and unconditional love are the foundation for your child's happiness.

Remember, making your child happy is not about fulfilling every desire or avoiding all negative experiences. It's about providing a nurturing and supportive environment, fostering emotional well-being, and guiding them towards personal growth and fulfilment. By debunking these myths and embracing the facts, you can better navigate the journey of fatherhood and contribute to your child's lasting happiness.

CHAPTER SEVEN

FATHER'S GUIDE: DECODING CHILDREN'S BEHAVIOURS AND BUILDING STRONG CONNECTIONS (25 COMMON TYPES OF BEHAVIOUR)

1. Withdrawal or reluctance to engage with the father:
- Lack of quality time spent together
- Inconsistent or unpredictable presence of the father
- Lack of emotional connection or bonding

2. Excessive clinginess or need for constant reassurance:
- Insecurity or fear of abandonment
- Absence or inconsistency in the father's presence
- Lack of trust in the father's availability or support

3. Aggressive behaviour towards the father:
- Witnessing aggression or conflict in the father's behaviour

- Lack of positive role modelling for managing anger and frustration
- Feeling threatened or unsafe in the father's presence

4. Difficulty expressing emotions or emotional shutdown:
- Lack of emotional openness or expression from the father
- Negative response or invalidation of emotions by the father
- Fear of vulnerability or judgement from the father

5. Seeking attention through negative behaviours:
- Lack of positive attention or engagement from the father
- Feeling ignored or neglected by the father
- Resorting to negative behaviours to elicit a response from the father

6. Development of anxious behaviours:
- Perceived inconsistency or unpredictability in the father's behaviour
- Lack of emotional reassurance or support from the father
- Overprotective or controlling behaviour from the father

7. Low self-esteem or self-worth:
- Lack of positive affirmation or validation from the father
- Criticism or belittling comments from the father
- Absence of healthy father-child interactions or bonding experiences

8. Difficulty in establishing healthy boundaries:
- Lack of clear boundaries set by the father
- Inconsistent enforcement of rules or consequences by the father
- Perceived invasion of personal space or autonomy by the father

9. Disinterest or detachment from family activities:
- Limited involvement or engagement from the father in family activities
- Lack of shared interests or quality time spent together
- Feeling disconnected or distant from the father

10. Attention-seeking behaviour or acting out:
- Craving for the father's attention and approval
- Feeling overlooked or invisible in the father's eyes
- Resorting to disruptive or challenging behaviours to gain the father's attention

11. Fear of failure or perfectionism:
- High expectations or pressure from the father to succeed
- Fear of disappointing or not meeting the father's standards
- Lack of support or encouragement from the father in the face of setbacks

12. Difficulty in trusting others:

- Betrayal or broken trust experienced in the father-child relationship
- Inconsistent or unreliable behaviour from the father
- Lack of emotional availability or openness from the father

13. Difficulty in forming healthy relationships:

- Lack of positive relationship modelling by the father
- Absence of healthy communication or conflict resolution skills demonstrated by the father
- Trust issues or fear of vulnerability stemming from the father-child relationship

14. Academic underachievement or lack of motivation:

- Lack of parental involvement or support in academic pursuits
- Limited emphasis on education or intellectual development from the father
- Absence of positive reinforcement or encouragement from the father

15. Resistant or defiant behaviour:

- Perceived lack of authority or consistency in the father's disciplinary approach
- Resistance to perceived unfairness or authoritarianism in the father's parenting style
- Lack of open communication or mutual respect between the father and child

16. Difficulty in managing emotions or impulsivity:

- Limited guidance or role modelling from the father on emotion regulation
- Lack of tools or strategies provided by the father to manage

16. Withdrawal or Avoidance:

- Cause: Lack of quality time spent with the father, resulting in a sense of emotional distance and disconnection.

17. Aggressive Behaviour:

- Cause: Unresolved conflicts or tensions between the child and father, leading to anger and frustration manifesting as aggression.

18. Seeking Attention:

- Cause: Craving for the father's attention and validation due to a perceived lack of acknowledgment or involvement.

19. Fear or Anxiety:

- Cause: Inadequate emotional support or reassurance from the father, leading to feelings of insecurity and fear.

20. Seeking Approval:

- Cause: A deep desire to gain the father's approval and acceptance, possibly due to feelings of inadequacy or the need for validation.

21. Emotional Instability:

- Cause: Lack of emotional guidance and stability from the father, resulting in difficulty managing and regulating emotions.

22. Academic Struggles:

- Cause: Limited involvement and support from the father in the child's academic pursuits, leading to a lack of motivation and guidance.

23. Trust Issues:

- Cause: Broken trust or inconsistency in the father's words and actions, resulting in difficulty trusting others and forming healthy relationships.

24. Low Self-Esteem:

- Cause: Lack of positive reinforcement and encouragement from the father, leading to feelings of inadequacy and low self-worth.

25. Attachment Issues:

- Cause: Insufficient bonding or attachment experiences with the father during early childhood, impacting the child's ability to form secure attachments later in life.

Please note that these points are general observations and not exhaustive. Each child is unique, and the causes behind their behaviours can vary.

CHAPTER EIGHT

My Father: A Personal Chapter

"My Father - A Testament of Love

My Father - A Beacon of Strength and Guidance

In the depths of my heart, there is a special place reserved for my father, the true hero of my life. As I reflect on the journey we have shared, I am overwhelmed with a profound sense of gratitude and admiration. This chapter is a heartfelt dedication to the man who has shaped me into the person I am today, an ode to his unwavering love, wisdom, and unwavering support.

My father, my guiding light, instilled in me the values that have become the cornerstone of my existence. He taught me the significance of integrity, honesty, and compassion. Through his own actions, he demonstrated the importance of living a life rooted in strong moral principles. I watched as he treated every person he encountered with kindness and respect, inspiring me to do the same. His unwavering belief in the power of empathy has fueled my own journey of understanding and connecting with others.

From the earliest days of my childhood, my father imparted in me the courage to face the world with resilience and determination. He taught me that strength lies not in the absence of fear, but in the ability to confront and overcome it. With his unwavering support, I learned to stand tall, even in the face of adversity. He instilled in me the confidence to pursue my dreams, to embrace challenges, and to never shy away from taking risks. Through his example, he showed me that true growth and self-discovery lie just beyond the boundaries of comfort.

The lessons of responsibility and hard work are etched deeply within my soul, thanks to my father's tireless efforts. He taught me the importance of giving weightage to my commitments and taking pride in the work I do. From the early morning hours when he would rise to provide for our family, to the late nights spent pouring over books to ensure our well-being, his dedication was unwavering. His tireless pursuit of excellence taught me that success is not handed to us but earned through perseverance, diligence, and unwavering determination.

As I embarked on my journey as a Homoeopathic practitioner, I carried with me the invaluable lessons my father had imparted. The sense of critical thinking, problem-solving, and compassion that guides my practice finds its roots in the teachings he bestowed upon me. His unwavering belief in the healing power of empathy and the importance of caring for others has shaped the very essence of my profession. I am forever grateful for the knowledge and wisdom he has bestowed upon me, enabling me to touch the lives of others and make a difference in the world of healthcare.

Words alone cannot express the depth of my appreciation for my father's presence in my life. I am privileged beyond measure to have him as my guiding light, my mentor, and my confidant. His unwavering love, support, and guidance have been the pillars that have sustained me through the ups and downs of life. Even in moments of solitude, I have never truly felt alone, for his love has been a constant presence, providing solace and strength.

In this book, I strive to shed light on the immense sacrifices and struggles that fathers endure in raising their children. Through the stories shared and the insights uncovered, I hope to inspire a deeper appreciation for the remarkable role fathers play in shaping the lives of their children. But amidst it all, I want to take this moment to dedicate these words to my own father, the true embodiment of a selfless, loving, and remarkable man.

With every word penned, every emotion expressed, and every sentiment shared, I want to honour my father for his unwavering love, guidance, and belief in me. I am forever grateful to the divine forces that have blessed me with him as my father. In this lifetime and in all the lives that may follow, I will always yearn for his presence, his wisdom, and his unwavering love.

Dad, this book is not only a testament to the trials and triumphs of fatherhood but also a heartfelt tribute to you. Thank you for shaping me into the person I am today, for teaching me the values that guide my path, and for being the unwavering source of strength in my life. You are my hero, my mentor, and my greatest inspiration. As I dedicate these words to you, I do so with profound love, gratitude, and an unwavering commitment to honour the legacy you have created.

To my father, the beacon of strength and guidance, this book is eternally dedicated.."

Conclusion

As we reach the end of this journey through the untold sufferings and sacrifices of fathers, I am reminded of the profound impact they have on our lives. Fathers, often silent heroes, navigate the complexities of fatherhood with love, dedication, and unwavering commitment. They shoulder the weight of responsibility, sacrifice their own desires, and selflessly provide for their families.

Through the stories shared in this book, we have witnessed the struggles, the triumphs, and the profound resilience of fathers. We have explored the depths of their emotions, their vulnerability, and their relentless pursuit of providing a better life for their children. We have uncovered the societal shadows that place expectations and stereotypes on fathers, and we have celebrated their unwavering love, support, and guidance.

In the words of Maya Angelou, "It's the courage to raise a child that makes you a father." This courage, demonstrated by fathers every day, is a testament to their strength and determination. They teach us life lessons, instil values, and lead by example. They inspire us to be better, to strive for greatness, and to find the courage within ourselves.

As we reflect on the journey of fatherhood, let us remember the words of Frederick Douglass, who said, "It is easier to build strong children than to repair broken men." The role of fathers in shaping the lives of their children is immeasurable. They have the power to mould and nurture, to instil confidence and resilience, and to create a foundation of love and support that will carry their children through life's challenges.

To all the fathers who have sacrificed, loved, and nurtured, I offer my deepest gratitude. Your dedication, your sacrifices, and your unwavering love are the threads that weave the tapestry of fatherhood. You are the unsung heroes who often go unnoticed, but your impact is imprinted on the hearts and souls of your children.

In closing, I invite you to reflect on the profound journey of fatherhood, not just through the lens of this book, but through your own experiences and connections. Cherish the fathers in your life, celebrate their triumphs, acknowledge their sacrifices, and offer them the love and gratitude they deserve.

Let us remember that the essence of fatherhood lies in the power of connection, in the bonds that transcend time and distance, and in the enduring love that shapes the lives of generations to come. As we honour the fathers who have walked this path, let us also recognize the importance of supporting and uplifting fathers everywhere, so that they may continue to flourish in their sacred role.

Thank you for joining me on this journey, and may the stories shared within these pages resonate in your hearts, inspire empathy, and serve as a tribute to the incredible fathers who make a difference in our lives.

With heartfelt gratitude,

Dr P Nidheesh